AF786804

ICSA Study Text

International Finance and Administration Qualifications

Accounting

ICSA Study Text

International Finance and
Administration Qualifications

Accounting

David Frederick

icsa
Trust through governance

First published 2015
Published by ICSA Publishing Ltd
Saffron House
6–10 Kirby Street
London EC1N 8TS

Typeset by Paul Barrett Book Production, Cambridge
Printed by Lightning Source

British Cataloguing in Publication Data
A catalogue record for this book is available from the British Library.

ISBN 978-1-86072-731-3

Contents

How to use this study text

ICSA study texts, developed to support ICSA's Level 4 International Finance and Administration Qualifications, follow a standard format and include a range of navigational, self-testing and illustrative features to help you get the most out of the support materials.

Each text is divided into three main sections:

- introductory material
- the text itself
- additional reference information.

The sections below show you how to find your way around the text and make the most of its features.

Introductory material

The introductory section of each text includes a full contents list and aims and learning outcomes for the modules in question.

Where relevant, the introductory section will also include a list of acronyms and abbreviations or a list of legal cases for reference.

The text itself

Each **part** opens with a list of the chapters to follow, an overview of what will be covered and learning outcomes for the part.

Every **chapter** opens with a list of the topics covered and an introduction specific to that chapter. Chapters are structured to allow students to break the content down into manageable sections for study. Each chapter ends with a summary of key content to reinforce understanding.

Features

The text is enhanced by a range of illustrative and self-testing features to assist understanding and to help you prepare for the examination. Each feature is presented in a standard format, so that you will become familiar with how to use them in your study.

These features are identified by a series of icons, as shown below.

The texts also include tables, figures and other illustrations as relevant.

Reference material

The text ends with a range of additional guidance and reference material, including a glossary of key terms, a directory of web resources and a comprehensive index.

Stop and think

Test yourself

Worked examples

Making it work

Case law

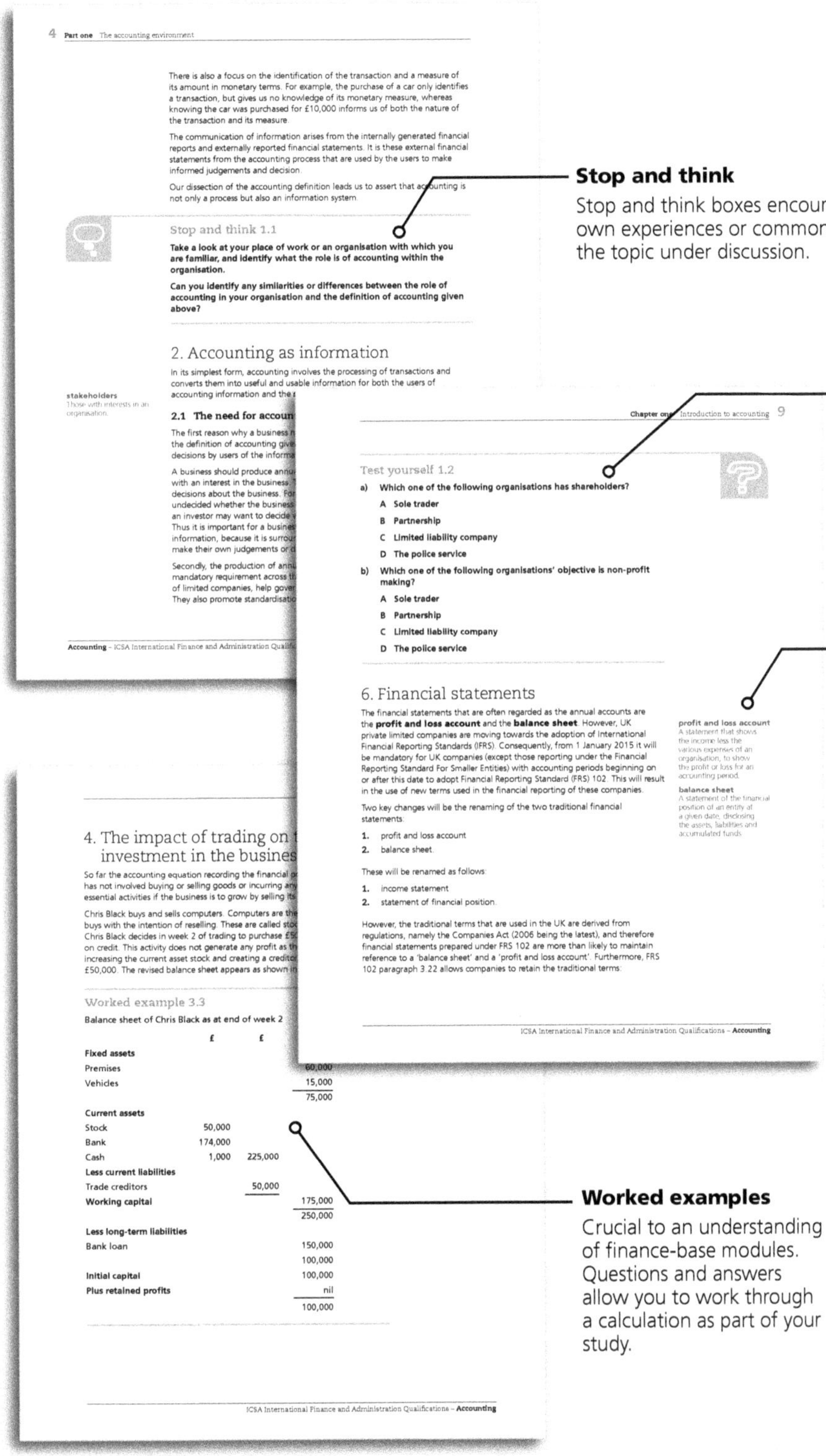

Stop and think

Stop and think boxes encourage you to reflect on how your own experiences or common business scenarios relate to the topic under discussion.

Test yourself

Short, revision-style questions to help you recap on key information and core concepts.

Definitions

Key terms are highlighted in bold on first use and defined in the page margins and the end-of-book glossary.

Worked examples

Crucial to an understanding of finance-base modules. Questions and answers allow you to work through a calculation as part of your study.

The Accounting modules

Aims

The accounting modules provides an introduction to the language of accounting, accounting conventions and the international framework of accounting. You will learn why financial information is produced, where it comes from, who uses it, and the purposes for which it is used.

Learning outcomes

On successful completion of these modules you will:

- know about the concept and purpose of accounting
- understand the needs of users of accounting information
- understand the main features of financial statements
- know about the accounting regulatory framework
- understand the accounting equation and how to classify capital, assets and liabilities
- understand the layout of financial statements and the impact of different transactions on the accounting equation
- be able to report business transactions
- be able to record the double entry for different business transactions
- know about adjustments made to ledger account balances before preparing financial statements
- understand the principles of accounting for fixed (non-current) assets
- understand internal controls within the double-entry bookkeeping system
- know how to prepare financial statements for a sole trader
- understand the format of financial statements of limited and public limited companies
- know how to prepare financial statements for not-for-profit organisations
- be able to interpret financial statements

A note on accounting regulation and terminology

The content and format of reporting financial information is governed by both national and international standards. For example, in the UK since January 2005, public limited companies have been required to present their financial statements using International Financial Reporting Standards (IFRS). However, private limited companies are not obliged to adopt IFRS and can produce financial statements governed by the local Financial Reporting Standards (FRS).

The Accounting modules require students to be aware of both tiers of reporting. Students at this level will not be required to prepare financial statements to comply with IFRS, but they will be required to extract and use financial information contained in IFRS-compliant financial statements.

Students should also be aware of some key differences of terminology used by the two tiers, including:

Financial Reporting Standards (FRS)	*International Financial Reporting Standards (IFRS)*
Profit and loss account	Income statement
Balance sheet	Statement of financial position
Fixed assets	Non-current assets
Long-term liabilities	Non-current liabilities
Stock	Inventory
Debtors	Receivables
Creditors	Payables

Past papers and practice questions

Students can access sample papers for these modules by logging into the MyICSA area of www.icsa.org.uk.

Acronyms and abbreviations

CPI	Consumer Price Index
FRS	Financial Reporting Standards
GPM	gross profit margin
GRN	goods received note
IAS	International Accounting Standard
IFRS	International Financial Reporting Standards
NBV	net book value
PDD	provision for doubtful debts
PPS	printing, postage and stationery

Part one

Chapter 1
Introduction to accounting

Chapter 2
Accounting regulatory framework

The accounting environment

Overview

This Part provides the conceptual framework around the subject of accounting and seeks to provide an operational definition and understanding of what is accounting and its purpose. The usefulness of the output of the accounting system is then explored, followed by an introduction to some of the terminology of accounting.

Chapter 2 provides an overview of the national and international standards, concepts and principles that provide the framework upon which the usefulness of accounting information is built.

Learning outcomes

At the end of this Part, you will:

- know about the concept and purpose of accounting
- understand the needs of users of accounting information
- understand the main features of financial statements
- know about the accounting regulatory framework.

Chapter one
Introduction to accounting

List of topics

1. What is accounting?
2. Accounting as information
3. Users of accounting information
4. Qualitative characteristics of accounting information
5. Business structures
6. Financial statements

Introduction

This chapter provides an overview of the purpose and role of accounting and accounting information in organisations for the benefit of those who use it to make economic decisions. In the examination of the purpose of accounting, the attributes of accounting information is discussed to enable those parties responsible for the preparation of accounting information to recognise and be aware of the requirements of accounting information for the user groups.

1. What is accounting?

Accounting systems, practices and procedures have become the cornerstone of every entity. However, it is necessary to provide students and readers with an understanding of the term 'accounting'.

An operational definition of the term has been obtained from the American Accounting Association, which defines accounting as 'the process of identifying, measuring and communicating economic information to permit informed judgements and decisions by users of the information'.

financial statements
A set of documents produced by a business to show financial performance and position of the business, including a trading profit and loss account and a balance sheet.

So, it is a process or set of interrelated procedures. These procedures span from recording the individual transactions to the preparation of the periodic **financial statements**.

There is also a focus on the identification of the transaction and a measure of its amount in monetary terms. For example, the purchase of a car only identifies a transaction, but gives us no knowledge of its monetary measure, whereas knowing the car was purchased for £10,000 informs us of both the nature of the transaction and its measure.

The communication of information arises from the internally generated financial reports and externally reported financial statements. It is these external financial statements from the accounting process that are used by the users to make informed judgements and decision.

Our dissection of the accounting definition leads us to assert that accounting is not only a process but also an information system.

Stop and think 1.1

Take a look at your place of work or an organisation with which you are familiar, and identify what the role is of accounting within the organisation.

Can you identify any similarities or differences between the role of accounting in your organisation and the definition of accounting given above?

2. Accounting as information

stakeholders
Those with interests in an organisation.

In its simplest form, accounting involves the processing of transactions and converts them into useful and usable information for both the users of accounting information and the **stakeholders** of the entity.

2.1 The need for accounts

The first reason why a business needs to produce accounts can be found in the definition of accounting given earlier: '...permit informed judgements and decisions by users of the information.'

A business should produce annual accounts because there will be parties with an interest in the business. These parties will be making judgements and decisions about the business. For example, a prospective employee may be undecided whether the business is one for whom they wish to work, whereas an investor may want to decide whether the business will be a good investment. Thus it is important for a business to produce accounts and accounting information, because it is surrounded by a variety of users who will need to make their own judgements or decisions about the business.

Secondly, the production of annual accounts for all or most business types is a mandatory requirement across the globe. Annual accounts, especially in the case of limited companies, help governments identify their corporation tax revenue. They also promote standardisation of reporting behaviour for businesses.

Thirdly, producing annual accounts is part of best practice for any business. The annual accounts provide a report on the performance of the business for an accounting period. It provides the business with an opportunity to reflect on its annual performance and communicates this to the wider community. As such, this has now become integrated as part of corporate governance best practice.

3. Users of accounting information

Accounting information is used by any individuals or groups involved in decision making. The principal individuals and groups who make decisions include the following.

- Managers are the people appointed to manage an organisation's day-to-day activities and operations. These individuals need information about the organisation's past, current and future financial position. This allows them to carry out the key elements of successful management – namely, planning and controlling their operations.
- Shareholders are the owners of the business who provide the money needed to start and keep the business operating. They may not be involved in the day-to-day operations of the business, but need to know if their business is making a profit, if that profit is satisfactory and how it is to be allocated.
- Lenders of finance want to know if their monies are safe. Lenders include banks, which provide long-term loans and need to be assured that the business will be able not only to make interest payments but also to repay the principal when required.
- Financial analysts include stockbrokers, financial advisers and financial journalists who want to be able to assess whether or not the business is a good investment. Financial analysts assess what potential profit investors can expect from their investment. This involves a review of accounting information provided from a number of sources such as the annual accounts and statements made to the media.
- Suppliers who provide goods and services to an organisation on credit want to know if they are going to be paid and how quickly. The financial information provides data on how long a company takes to pay its bills.
- Government bodies, such as the local and national taxation authorities, need some idea of how much taxation the organisation owes. This allows government bodies to plan how much they have to spend and to ensure that accounting records comply with the law. The government also uses accounting information for the regulation of industry and compilation of national statistics.
- Customers who are going to do business with an organisation want to know if it is financially able to continue in existence. It is essential that a customer who purchases goods or services from the organisation has confidence that they will be able to have a regular supply of those goods and services. Customers may also be in a dependency relationship if they have product warranties/guarantees or need replacement of specialist parts.

- Employees rely on the organisation to provide their principal source of regular income. They use financial information to assess their job security and the organisation's ability to make pay awards. Similarly, past employees are interested in their pensions, while potential employees may require accounting information to assist their decision to join an organisation.
- The general public are likely to be members of any of the groups mentioned above; for example, they may be employees and customers of the organisation. However, in their role as members of the general public, they are likely to have a wider interest in the financial performance of an organisation. Thus they might be interested to know if the business is spending sufficient money to protect the environment from damage caused by the business's production processes.

4. Qualitative characteristics of financial information

If financial statements are to be useful to those who read and use the information they provide, they must satisfy certain criteria. The Conceptual Framework for Financial Reporting separates the qualitative characteristics of financial information into fundamental and enhancing characteristics, as shown in Figure 1.1.

Fundamental characteristics:	1. Relevance 2. Faithful representation
Enhancing characteristics:	1. Comparability 2. Verifiability 3. Timeliness 4. Understandability

Figure 1.1: Qualitative characteristics of financial information

The two fundamental characteristics are as follows:

- **Relevance**: Financial information exhibits the characteristics of relevance when it can make a difference to the decisions that are made its users. In addition, for the financial information to be capable of making a difference it must also exhibit a predictive and/or confirmatory value. An example of the predictive and confirmatory value of financial information is sales revenue of an entity. The current year's sales revenue can be used to forecast next year's performance or to compare the forecast made for the current year in the previous reporting period.
- **Faithful representation**: Financial information should represent economic phenomena in a complete, neutral and error-free state. As a result, the reader and/or user of the financial information has a complete picture of the phenomena to make their decision. Furthermore, a faithful representation in isolation does not provide useful information.

These fundamental characteristics are supported by four enhancing characteristics, which serve to aid the usefulness of the financial information that is presented in financial statements to readers and users.

- **Comparability**: Comparability is the qualitative characteristic that enables users to identify and understand similarities in, and differences among, items within the financial statements of a reporting entity. Consequently, for comparability to exist there must be at least two reported items.
- **Verifiability**: Verifiability enables that different knowledgeable and independent observers reach a consensus on whether a particular presentation of an economic phenomena has been faithfully represented. The verification may be direct or indirect. Direct verification is verification via direct observation, for example, a physical stock count. Indirect verification may be conducted using the inputs to a financial model, formula or other technique and recalculating the outputs using the same methodology. An example is verifying the carrying amount of inventory by checking the inputs (quantities and costs) and recalculating the ending inventory using the same cost-flow assumption (for example, using the first-in, first-out method).
- **Timeliness**: The ability to provide users with financial information to be able to influence their decision-making process. In general, the older the information, the less useful it will be to the users. However, it may be the case that older information is not discarded because users require it to examine and assess trends in the behaviour of some items within financial statements.
- **Understandability**: Financial information that has been classified, characterised and presented in a clear and concise manner is deemed to be understandable. The exclusion of information because of its degree of complexity to enhance understandability renders such information to be incomplete and misleading for the purpose of its users.

The qualitative characteristic of materiality has not become redundant in the Conceptual Framework but a recognition that materiality is an entity-specific feature of relevance. It is not possible to provide general terms to address each case of materiality, as materiality is dependent upon the nature or magnitude of the item to which the financial information relates. In essence, the issue of materiality should be examined on a case-by-case basis.

Test yourself 1.1

a) **Which one of the following is a fundamental characteristic of financial information?**

   A Verifiability

   B Relevance

   C Understandability

   D Timeliness

b) **Identify six groups who might be interested in the financial information of a public company.**

c) **Discuss their interest in the financial information of a public company.**

5. Business structures

There are three principal business structures:

1. sole trader
2. partnership
3. limited liability company.

5.1 Sole trader

sole trader
A person carrying on business with sole legal responsibility for the business, not in partnership or as a company.

A **sole trader** is a single individual who sets up in business on their own. The individual has sole responsibility for all the affairs of the business and has unlimited liability for all the debts of the business. As the sole owner, the individual benefits from owning all of any annual profit generated by the business.

5.2 Partnership

partnership
A business where ownership is shared among two or more people.

A **partnership** is where two or more persons form a business. Each partner will own a share of the business and a share of any liability for any debts that the business may incur. Each partner will also receive a share of the profits as per the partnership agreement. In the absence of such an agreement, profits and/or losses will be shared equally in accordance with the provisions of the Partnership Act 1890.

5.3 Limited liability company

limited company
A business owned by shareholders with their liability limited to their share capital.

A limited liability company is a separate legal entity owned by shareholders and managed by directors. These can be the same people. The capital of the company is divided into shares which have a fixed value per share. To become a member or shareholder of a **limited company**, an individual must buy one or more shares. Once the shareholder has paid for their share(s), their liability for the company's debts is limited to those shares.

Thus if a limited company loses all its assets, the maximum liability of the shareholder is the value of their shares.

Each type of business is subject to different levels of regulation and legislation. For example, in the UK, all types of business have to maintain records for taxation purposes which can be inspected by Her Majesty's Revenue & Customs (HMRC).

It is not only the three commercial entities discussed here that produce annual accounts. Non-commercial organisations whose objectives are usually non-profit making also produce annual accounts. Examples of non-commercial organisations may include sports clubs, charitable organisations and public sector organisations.

Test yourself 1.2

a) **Which one of the following organisations has shareholders?**

- **A** **Sole trader**
- **B** **Partnership**
- **C** **Limited liability company**
- **D** **The police service**

b) **Which one of the following organisations' objective is non-profit making?**

- **A** **Sole trader**
- **B** **Partnership**
- **C** **Limited liability company**
- **D** **The police service**

6. Financial statements

The financial statements that are often regarded as the annual accounts are the **profit and loss account** and the **balance sheet**. However, UK private limited companies since 1 January 2015 have moved towards International Financial Reporting Standards (IFRS) with the introduction of a new suite of UK Financial Reporting Standards (FRS).

profit and loss account
A statement that shows the income less the various expenses of an organisation, to show the profit or loss for an accounting period.

balance sheet
A statement of the financial position of an entity at a given date, disclosing the assets, liabilities and accumulated funds.

Since 1 January 2015 it has been mandatory for UK companies except micro entities (see Chapter 10) to Financial Reporting Standards to (FRS) 102. Micro entities saw the arrival on 1 January 2016 of their own reporting standard Financial Reporting Standards (FRS) 105. The arrival of Financial Reporting Standards to (FRS) 102 resulted in the use of new terms used in the financial reporting of these companies.

Two key changes will be the renaming of the two traditional financial statements:

1. profit and loss account

2. balance sheet.

These will be renamed as follows:

1. income statement

2. statement of financial position.

However, the traditional terms that are used in the UK are derived from regulations, namely the Companies Act (2006 being the latest), and therefore financial statements prepared under FRS 102 and 105 are more than likely to maintain reference to a 'balance sheet' and a 'profit and loss account'. Furthermore, FRS 102 paragraph 3.22 allows companies to retain the traditional terms:

An entity may use titles for the financial statements other than those used in this FRS as long as they are not misleading.

FRS 102 para 3.22

6.1 Profit and loss account

The profit and loss account is a statement that shows the annual performance of the business. The performance is measured in terms of the accounting profit for the accounting period. Accounting profit is derived from the matching of the income receivable for the accounting period against the expenses incurred during the accounting period. The result is either a profit or a loss. When the income receivable exceeds the expenses incurred, an accounting profit is generated. Conversely, when the expenses incurred exceeds the income receivable, an accounting loss is generated.

6.2 Balance sheet

The balance sheet provides a summary of the position of a business at a set date in time. It provides a list of what the business owns (assets) and what the business owes (liabilities). These terms will be fully explained in later chapters.

6.3 Business transactions

Business transactions can be separated into four parts, as shown in Figure 1.2. Transactions are either expenditure or income. In addition, transactions may be capital or revenue in nature. It is necessary to explain the distinction between capital income and revenue income, and capital expenditure and revenue expenditure.

Revenue income	Capital income
Revenue expenditure	Capital expenditure

Figure 1.2: Business transactions

Capital and revenue expenditure

Accountants have to distinguish or classify expenditure (and income) into capital and revenue.

capital expenditure
Expenditure that is likely to provide a benefit to the organisation for more than one accounting period/financial year.

Capital expenditure is expenditure that is likely to provide a benefit to the organisation for more than one accounting period/financial year. The key points are as follows.

- The benefits and period of those benefits may be difficult to predict.
- Such expenditure can be defined as increasing the earning capacity of the business.

- Capital expenditure is incurred on the purchase of fixed assets such as land and buildings, plant and machinery, vehicles and fixtures and fittings. The cost of these fixed assets is, therefore, accounted for over their anticipated useful life.
- Capital expenditure usually involves an annual depreciation (loss in value) charge.
- Capital expenditure is concerned with purchasing high-value, long-term and permanent fixed assets for use in the business. These assets are not bought to be resold.

Revenue expenditure is expenditure that is necessary for the day-to-day operations of the business. The key points are as follows.

revenue expenditure
Expenditure on the supply and manufacture of goods and provision of services charged in the accounting period in which they are consumed.

- It is expenditure that is likely to provide benefit to the organisation for only the current accounting/financial year and so is charged against profits in the period to which it relates.
- It is a cost used by the organisation in trading.
- Revenue expenditure includes, but is not restricted to, running costs such as electricity, business rates, wages and salaries of employees, interest charges, and purchase of consumables such as stationery and goods purchased for resale.

Capital and revenue income

Commercial organisations generally engage in trade with the objective of generating a profit. This is usually made possible through the purchase and sale of goods and services. Generally the proceeds from a sale are classified as income. However, the top half of Figure 1.2 indicates that income, just like expenditure, can be subdivided into two types: capital and revenue.

Capital income is the proceeds from the sale of capital items and non-trading activities. The key points are as follows.

capital income
The proceeds of selling fixed assets.

- It is income derived from the trade in the long-term assets of the organisation.
- It is income outside of the normal trading activities of the organisation.
- Capital income includes the sale of tangible fixed assets, fixed asset investments, government grants and the introduction of fresh money to help the business grow. The profit or loss from the sale is transferred to the profit and loss account for the accounting period when the sale took place.
- The profit or loss from the sale is not regarded as part of the operational profit and loss.

Revenue income is derived from the provision of goods and services falling within the business's ordinary activities, after deduction of returns, trade discounts and value added tax; it is also called turnover/sales. The key points are as follows.

revenue income
Amounts derived from the provision of goods and services falling within the company's ordinary activities, after deduction of returns, trade discounts and value added tax; also called turnover/sales.

- It is income derived from the organisation's normal trading activities.
- It is the principal income source for trading and commercial organisations.

- Revenue income includes income from the sale of goods to customers, rents received, dividends received, interest received, etc.

Importance of the distinction

The distinction between capital and revenue items is critical. If capital and revenue items are not classified accurately, the accounting profit will be incorrectly calculated. For example, if a capital expenditure item is included as revenue expenditure, then the annual profit will be understated. Similarly, if a capital grant were included in one year's accounts, then the annual profits would be overstated.

Test yourself 1.3

a) Which one of the following expenditure by a business would be classified as capital expenditure?

A £4,000 spent on advertising

B £7,500 spent on loan interest

C £15,000 spent on plant and equipment

D £20,000 spent on premises insurance

b) Explain what capital expenditure is and what revenue expenditure is.

c) List the two fundamental characteristics of financial information.

d) Explain comparability and verifiability of financial information.

Chapter summary

- Accounting information is not an end in itself, but is produced to assist the users of the information in making decisions.
- The effectiveness of financial information is determined by various characteristics.
- The characteristics of financial information is separated into fundamental and enhancing characteristics.
- The principal financial statements are the profit and loss account and the balance sheet.
- FRS 102 has been introduced to move UK company financial reporting towards harmonisation with International Financial Reporting Standards.
- The profit and loss account reveals the annual performance over the year measured in terms of a profit or loss.
- The balance sheet provides the financial position of a business at a set date in time.

- Income and expenditure are separated between capital and revenue.
- Capital is non-trading transactions with an impact on the organisation beyond one year.
- Revenue transactions are operational transactions reported in the profit and loss account of a business.

Test yourself answers

Test yourself 1.1

a) B – Relevance.

b) Any six of the following stakeholders would be interested in the financial information of a public limited company: managers, shareholders, lenders, financial analysts, suppliers, government bodies, customers, employees, the general public.

c)

Stakeholders	Interest in the financial information of public company
Managers	Operational activities and affairs of the company. The company's past, current and future financial position.
Shareholders	The financial success or viability of the company, as this determines the scope for returns on their investment.
Lenders	The viability of the company, as this determines its ability to repay its short- and long-term debts.
Financial analysts	The performance of the company, as this is reported to the wider investment community.
Suppliers	The company's ability to pay for any goods supplied on credit and also the scope for future sales to the company.
Government bodies	The scope for tax revenues and also the wider public policy planning, such as employment opportunities and economic growth.
Customers	A regular and continuous supply of their goods and services; confidence that goods can be returned if they are defective.
Employees	The security and reliability of their employment and future income stream to finance their current and future plans.
General public	The social, environmental and economic impact a company has upon the community.

Test yourself 1.2

a) C – Limited liability company

b) D – The police service

Test yourself 1.3

a) C – £15,000 spent on plant and equipment

b) Capital expenditure is expenditure on an item that has a lifespan beyond one accounting year and its cost is spread over its useful economic life, such as expenditure on property, plant and equipment.

   Revenue expenditure is expenditure on an item that has a lifespan of less than one accounting year and its cost is charged to the profit and loss account, such as salaries, administration or accountancy fees.

c) Relevance and faithful representation.

d) Comparability is the qualitative characteristic that enables users to identify and understand similarities in, and differences among, items within the financial statements of a reporting entity. Consequently for comparability to exist, there must be at least two reported items.

   Verifiability enables different knowledgeable and independent observers to reach a consensus on whether a particular presentation of an economic phenomena has been faithfully represented. The verification may be direct or indirect. Direct verification is verification via direct observation, for example, a physical stock count. Indirect verification may be conducted using the inputs to a financial model, formula or other technique and recalculating the outputs using the same methodology. An example is verifying the carrying amount of inventory by checking the inputs (quantities and costs) and recalculating the ending inventory using the same cost flow assumption (for example, using the first-in, first-out method).

Chapter two
Accounting regulatory framework

List of topics

1. Accounting regulation
2. Accounting concepts and conventions
3. Basic accounting concepts
4. Other accounting concepts

Introduction

This chapter provides an overview of the principal regulations, rules and guidelines that govern our understanding of the content and reporting of accounting financial information. The remainder of the chapter identifies and outlines the accounting concepts upon which modern financial reporting is based.

1. Accounting regulation

The regulation of accounting has evolved over time. Today, the content and format of reporting financial information is governed by national and international standards. This two-tier approach to the governance of financial information reporting has emerged since the birth of the first International Financial Reporting Standard in June 2003. Since this date, many countries have adopted **International Financial Reporting** Standards (IFRS). The UK moved towards harmonisation with IFRS in stages. From January 2005, **public listed companies** were required to present their financial statements using IFRS, whilst private limited companies were allowed to follow UK Generally Accepted Accounting Practice (GAAP). However, 1 January 2015 saw the arrival of a new suite of UK Financial Reporting Standards (FRS 100, 101 and 102). The adoption of these Financial Reporting Standards were mandatory for UK private limited companies, unless they met the criteria for being classified as a micro entity. The adoption of UK Financial Reporting Standards was completed on 1 January 2016 with micro entities having to adopt Financial Reporting Standard 105 for their financial reporting. The Accounting syllabus requires students to be aware of the different tiers of reporting. However, students at this level will not be required to prepare financial statements to comply with IFRS or UK FRS 100, 101, 102 or 105. Students will be required to be familiar with the terminology

International Financial Reporting Standards
A set of principles-based standards, interpretations and framework for financial statements.

public listed companies
Limited companies whose shares are available to be purchased by the general public.

and will be required to extract and use financial information presented in these financial statements.

Students can find a fuller discussion of the format of the financial statements required to comply with UK Financial Reporting Standard 102 and 105 in Chapter 10.

Additional regulation in the UK is provided by the:

- Companies Act 2006; and
- requirements of the London Stock Exchange.

going concern
The assumption that the entity will continue in operational existence for the foreseeable future.

accruals
Costs that have not so far been taken into account at the end of a period because they have not yet been invoiced but are to be invoiced in arrears – for example, gas or electricity.

prudence
The principle that income is included in the financial statements only when realised, while likely losses are included as soon as possible.

consistency
The principle that there is uniformity of accounting treatment of like items within each accounting period and from one period to the next.

1.1 Financial Reporting Standards (FRS)

The Financial Reporting Standards set out the principles that should underlie the preparation and the terminology to be adopted in the presentation of general purpose financial statements. FRS 18 Accounting Policies identified the **going concern** and **accruals** concepts as the bedrock of accounting. The **prudence** and **consistency** concepts were termed 'desirable qualities of financial information' (FRS 18).

1.2 International Financial Reporting Standards (IFRS)

The International Financial Reporting Standards provide an international framework for the preparation and presentation of financial statements. The framework is a set of principles-based general rules plus some prescriptive treatments.

The IFRS identified four underlying concepts:

1. accrual basis;
2. going concern;
3. stable measuring unit; and
4. units of constant purchasing power.

Test yourself 2.1

a) **What are the desirable elements of financial statements?**

b) **What are the bedrock principles of financial statements?**

c) **What are the two underlying accounting concepts found in the IFRS but not in the FRS?**

2. Accounting concepts and conventions

Understanding accounting information would be relatively easy if every number in the information were verifiable by tangible evidence – for example, if the economic value placed on every piece of equipment and building could be verified by reference to the historic cost of the equipment as revealed by the relevant invoice. In reality, many pieces of accounting information are based on personal judgements – in other words, they are subjective. The piece of equipment referred to above might be valued subjectively in accounting statements at replacement price.

In order to provide a framework for these subjective judgements, the accounting profession has developed accounting concepts, conventions and standards. These are the rules financial accountants and auditors are expected to comply with when preparing financial statements. These concepts underpin both the FRS and IFRS discussed above. The concepts and standards aim to increase the objectivity of the methods used to record the business activities in financial statements.

3. Basic accounting concepts

The production of accounts follows four basic concepts. These are the two pairs of concepts termed 'bedrock and desirable concepts' in FRS 18, described above:

1. going concern
2. accruals or matching
3. prudence
4. consistency.

3.1 The going concern concept

The going concern concept is the assumption that the business will continue to operate in the foreseeable future – that there is no intention to close it and no intention to make significant cutbacks to the nature of the business. This approach means that the information provided by financial statements is most relevant.

The implication of this concept is that the **assets** of a business, such as buildings and equipment, will normally be valued at their historic cost, i.e. their original purchase cost. The issue here is that the assets of the business should not be valued at their break-up value, i.e. the amount they would sell for if they were to be sold one by one and over a relatively short period of time. The break-up values tend not to be relevant to the users of accounts, who are assuming that the business will continue to operate over the remaining useful life of the asset. As an example, if a business acquires machinery at a cost of £100,000 which is expected to last five years, it is usual to **write off** the cost of the asset over the five-year period against the profits to which the asset has contributed.

asset
Any tangible or intangible possession that has value.

write off
Reduce the value of an asset to nil on a balance sheet.

This practice of writing off the cost of a long-term asset over its useful life helps to ensure that as the asset deteriorates physically or operationally, its value in the accounting records is reduced to reflect that loss. This is done over the life of the asset because it would be inappropriate to charge the full purchase cost to any single accounting period. The profit would be understated for that period, while in subsequent periods the profit would be overstated. Equally, to show the asset at nil value in the accounts would be misleading, as it would imply either no asset or a valueless asset. The accountant must therefore have evidence that

depreciation
The measure of wearing out, consumption or other reduction in the useful economic life of a fixed asset.

the asset will last beyond the end of the year. The yearly reduction in the cost of the asset is called **depreciation** and appears as one of the expenses in the profit and loss account. Depreciation is dealt with more fully in Chapter 7.

The going concern concept applies to other assets such as stock and debtors (customers who owe the business money for goods or services provided) where a similar assumption regarding the sale of stock or the collection of the debt applies.

The concept can also be applied to long-term loans or liabilities owed by the business. If the going concern concept were not applied, it is likely that these would become payable immediately and classed as short-term debts or liabilities.

The assumption that the business is a going concern really justifies the use of the historic cost concept, which in turn emphasises the high importance given to the qualities of objectivity and verifiability in accounting data.

3.2 The accruals concept

accounting period
The period for which the financial statements have been prepared.

This concept works on the principle that revenues and costs are matched with each other and dealt with in the profit and loss account of the **accounting period** to which they relate, irrespective of the period of actual receipt or payment.

Profit is measured not by comparing cash received during the financial period with cash spent, but by matching expenditure incurred with income earned.

The accruals concept states that when computing profit, the sales income (or sales revenue) earned should be matched only against the expenditure incurred when earning it.

revenue recognition concept
The recording of revenue in the books of accounts in the appropriate accounting period. Revenue is recognised when the buyer assumes ownership and title of the goods.

This raises the question of when sales revenue (or income) should be recorded in the accounts. If goods are sold on credit, or deferred payment terms, when should the revenue be shown? Traditionally, the question is answered by reference to the realisation or **revenue recognition concept**. The prudence concept stresses that sales revenue should be 'realised' and 'recognised' only when a critical event has occurred. This event would normally be when:

- a cash sale is made; or
- the goods are delivered or the services provided, and not when the sale proceeds are received. This will normally coincide with the date on the invoice or the date of delivery if the issue of the invoice is delayed.

The accruals concept refers to this critical event as the point in time when the revenue is earned.

The accruals concept is extended to the area of expenditure or costs. Costs should be recognised as arising when they are incurred and not when the cash is paid. For example, where an annual insurance premium is paid in advance and spreads across two financial years, care has to be taken that each financial year takes the appropriate share of the premium. Where an amount paid in this financial year relates to the next financial year, there is a **prepayment**, or a payment in advance, which will be carried forward to be charged in the subsequent year's accounts. This avoids the accounting period when the insurance premium is paid incurring the cost of another accounting period.

prepayment
Expenditure on goods or services for future benefit, which is to be charged to future operations, e.g. rentals paid in advance.

Alternatively, some services – for example, telephone, gas and electricity – are seen as being incurred or used on the date they are received. At the end of a financial year these services have been consumed or incurred, but no invoice has been received by the company. The business will treat these as **accrued expenses** or expenses owing.

accrued expense
An expense that has been incurred and the benefit received during an accounting period which remains unpaid at the end of the accounting period.

In practice the accruals concept shows profit/loss as follows:

Revenue earned – Expenditure incurred = Profit (or loss) for an accounting period

3.3 The prudence concept

This is the principle that income is included in the financial statements only when realised, while likely losses are included as soon as possible.

The prudence concept means that where a selection has to be made between different procedures or valuations, the one selected should be that which gives the most cautious presentation of the financial position or results of the business. It also follows that where a loss can be foreseen, it should be recognised and taken into account immediately.

The prudence concept reflects the traditional tendency for accountants to recognise likely losses as soon as possible, but to defer recognition of potential income until it arises. The use of the prudence concept can be observed in the case of stock. Accepted accounting practice states that stock should be valued at the lower of historic cost and net realisable value. Thus if the stock is likely to be sold for less than was originally paid for it, a loss will be made. The accountant recognises this loss immediately by reducing the value of unsold stock to net realisable value. This concept is sometimes called 'conservatism'.

There are at least two reasons for following the prudence concept, namely:

1. 'understating' profit looks after the traditional interests of creditors and bankers; and
2. a conservative approach may counteract the natural optimism of some managers and owners.

3.4 The consistency concept

It was stressed earlier that some accounting information is verifiable by tangible evidence and as such is objective. In contrast, many pieces of accounting information are based on personal judgements, i.e. they are subjective.

The consistency principle is based on a uniformity of accounting treatment of like items within each accounting period and from one period to the next.

In certain important areas – for example, in the valuation of stocks or the estimation of bad debts – a company has a choice of several equally valid methods. These have different effects on reported profits from year to year. Firms may be tempted to take advantage of these alternatives to show an apparent 'improvement' in their financial performance or strength. The use of the consistency concept provides a barrier to this being easily done.

Accordingly, once a company chooses a particular accounting treatment for an item, it must be applied consistently within each accounting period and from one period to the next for similar items. For example, it is assumed that the method of valuing closing stock is the same as that used to value opening stock. This does not mean that the company is not allowed to change its accounting methods. It may, provided that there are good reasons for doing so. However, if it does, the effect on that year's profits should be highlighted in the financial statements to facilitate comparisons with previous years.

One aim of applying the consistency concept is to increase the usefulness of accounting information. The information can be compared with similar information about the company for some other period or point in time, and with similar information about other businesses.

Test yourself 2.2

a) **Explain the consistency concept.**

b) **Provide an example to demonstrate the going concern concept.**

c) **What accounting concept is also known as the conservatism concept?**

4. Other accounting concepts

The four accounting concepts already described are widely viewed as being basic to the preparation and content of accounting information. However, there are other principles/concepts that the accountant uses in the preparation of financial statements.

4.1 The materiality concept

materiality
The principle that financial statements should disclose items separately that are significant enough to affect evaluation or decisions.

Materiality refers to the relative significance or importance of a particular matter in the context of the financial statements as a whole. A matter is material if its omission or misstatement would reasonably influence the decisions of a user of the accounts.

An item in the accounts that is too trivial to affect a user's understanding of the financial statements is referred to as immaterial. When preparing financial statements, it is important to assess what is material and what is not, so that resources are not wasted in the pursuit of excessive detail. Thus a low-value office clock or paper shredder may last for several years but is highly unlikely to be subject to an annual depreciation charge, because it is not worth the effort of keeping such detailed records.

There is no absolute measure of materiality. Often a rule of thumb will be applied such as defining material items as those with, say, a value greater than 5% of the profit disclosed by the accounts, but it is really a question of judgement. In making the assessment of materiality, both the amount and the context in which it appears must be considered. For example, 5% of £5 million profits can hardly be regarded as trivial.

Stop and think 2.1

The following statements have been extracted from the published accounts of a business.

'The financial statements are prepared on the going concern basis unless it is inappropriate to presume that the company will continue in existence.'

'The accounts include judgements and estimates that are reasonable and prudent.'

Explain the meaning of the above statements with reference to your accounting concepts.

4.2 The money measurement concept

The **money measurement concept** states that accounts will deal only with those items to which a monetary value can be attached. As we have seen, this is fairly straightforward in that the value can be taken from a source document such as an invoice. Thus if a company purchases a vehicle or an item of stock, or uses electricity, the value can be taken from the relevant invoices. Such values may be easily attributed to assets such as machinery and equipment, but other assets such as managerial skills or workforce loyalty may be difficult to quantify. Because they cannot be evaluated in monetary terms, they do not normally appear in the accounts.

money measurement concept
The principle that financial accounting information relates only to those activities that can be expressed in money terms.

4.3 The business entity concept

The principle that financial accounting information relates only to the activities of the business entity and not to the activities of its owner(s).

The **business entity concept** means that accountants regard a business as a separate entity, distinct from its owners or managers. Company law recognises this by viewing the company as a separate legal entity independent of its directors and shareholders. Accountants also regard a sole proprietorship or partnership in the same way, but only for accounting purposes.

business entity concept
The principle that financial accounting information relates only to the activities of the business entity and not to the activities of its owner(s).

The distinction is important because the accountant is trying to measure the financial performance of the business and therefore needs to exclude the private assets and liabilities of the owner.

4.4 Historic cost concept

The principle that resources are normally stated in accounts at the amount that was paid to acquire them.

historic cost concept
The principle that resources are normally stated in accounts at the amount that was paid to acquire them.

The **historic cost concept** is the basic principle of accounting that resources are normally stated in accounts at the amount the business paid to acquire them. This ensures that the objectivity of accounts is improved as there is supporting independent evidence, such as an invoice, to verify an asset's purchase price or the amount paid for an expense. Objectivity is important as it prevents the accountant or management from influencing the financial performance of the business by deciding on a value independently.

The use of valuations is to be avoided where possible. Valuations may be regarded as subjective, so accountants prefer to deal with historic costs. Valuations also tend to vary according to what the valuation is to be used for and may include many assumptions.

On the other hand, while historic costs are objectively verifiable, they tend to be less useful in periods of inflation. Individual assets, such as land or property, tend to appreciate in value significantly while other assets, such as vehicles, tend to depreciate. For these reasons it is common to prepare modified historic cost accounts. This means that periodically, companies include more up-to-date valuations for some of their assets. This is referred to as modified historic cost.

4.5 Stable monetary unit

stable monetary unit concept
The use of monetary units to report items in financial statements. This permits nominal comparative analysis, although the monetary unit may not maintain a constant value.

The **stable monetary unit concept** requires financial statements to be expressed in monetary units. For example, for international comparative purposes, financial statements are often expressed in terms of US dollars ($). The use of a monetary unit as a basis in the presentation of financial statements assumes the currency remains constant between accounting periods. Changing price levels (inflation) often signifies a change in the monetary unit value between accounting periods.

4.6 Units of constant purchasing power

units of constant purchasing power concept
During exceptional periods of hyperinflation, all non-monetary items are to be restated in terms of the consumer price index as at the end of the accounting period. This seeks to maintain the capital purchasing power during inflationary and deflationary periods.

The **units of constant purchasing power concept** requires all non-monetary items (variable and constant real value non-monetary items) in historical cost or current cost period-end financial statements to be restated in terms of the period-end Consumer Price Index (CPI) during exceptional periods of hyperinflation. The constant purchasing power seeks to maintain the financial capital purchasing power during periods of inflation and deflation.

4.7 Objectivity

The objectivity concepts states that the production and analysis of accounting information by accounting professionals is conducted in a non-biased manner. The accounts are prepared without recourse to any personal opinion of the entity, thus being free of bias and prejudice. This is maintained and supported through the use of national and international accounting standards plus the report of the auditor.

4.8 Realisation

This is the principle that states that profit is only recognised when it has been realised. Only realised profits should be included in financial statements.
FRS 18 provides the following explanation:

> In preparing financial statements, an entity will have regard to requirements in companies legislation that only profits realized at the balance sheet date should be included in the profit and loss account. Companies legislation requires realized profits to be determined in accordance with principles generally accepted at the time that financial statements are prepared.
>
> Para 28, p16 FRS, 18 Dec 2000

A notable exception to this principle has been the treatment for land and buildings. It has become commonly accepted that land and buildings are revalued periodically to reflect their current value. This is often performed to provide a more meaningful balance sheet and to deter acquisition for asset stripping. The revaluation of land and buildings generates an unrealised profit. This unrealised profit is never credited to the profit and loss account, because it is unrealised. The unrealised profit is credited to a revaluation account, which forms part of the capital reserves or non-distributable reserves.

4.9 Duality

This is the principle that states that for every transaction there is a debit and credit book entry. Duality is the cornerstone of the accounting process. Every transaction has two book entries: a donor account (value losing) and a receiver account (value added). The donor account is known as the 'credit' and the receiver account is the 'debit'. It is traditional to refer to the debit account first when recording accounting transactions. An example of the duality principle is the purchase of an asset for cash. The asset account would be the receiver account, i.e. the debit, and the bank account would be the donor account, i.e. the credit. This can be written as follows:

Debit	Asset account
Credit	Bank account

The recording of transactions will be examined in Chapter 5.

4.10 Substance over form

Substance over form requires that when accounting for transactions, they should be presented with reference to their economic substance and not their legal form. An example is the purchase of a fixed asset on hire purchase. The legal ownership does not pass to the purchaser until the final payment has been made. However, the accounting substance would be to recognise the fixed asset in the accounts from the date of the hire purchase agreement.

substance over form
Transactions are accounted for by their commercial reality rather than legal form.

4.11 Periodicity

periodicity concept
The period for which a set of business activities is reported in the financial statement.

The **periodicity concept** requires that an entity reports its activity at set time intervals. The reporting period is usually 12 months but it can be more frequent, such as quarterly, bi-annually or monthly, subject to the desire of the entity and the requirements of the users of the financial statements. Using equal reporting periods permits comparability between accounting periods. Two of the most popular accounting reporting period year-ends are 30 June and 31 December.

5. The changing UK tax horizon

In 2015 the UK government announced a major initiative to improve the effectiveness and efficiency of the UK tax system, Making Tax Digital. The objective was to transform the UK tax system through digitalisation of record keeping, reporting and updating for income tax, VAT and corporation tax. The initiative was planned to commence in April 2018. However, following consultation and an awareness of the magnitude of the initiative, the MTD start date has been postponed until April 2019. Moreover, when it does commence in April 2019, it will only be with the VAT reporting, with the other taxes to follow in 2020.

This is the greatest transformation planned for the UK tax system since the birth of self-assessment on 6th April 1996. However, there is still a lack of clarity and certainty about the face of MTD and its operation across the sector. All that is known is that change is coming to the UK tax system, but its exact nature and scale is less clear.

Test yourself 2.3

a) **Which accounting concept is concerned with accounting information being produced in a non-biased manner?**

b) **What accounting concept is demonstrated by the double entry system?**

c) **Is the following statement true or false? Profit is recognised when payment is received for the transaction.**

Chapter summary

- Organisations have to comply with a range of regulations and legislation.
- Accounting regulation is in two tiers: national and international
- National standards have a tendency to follow the international standards.
- International regulation is derived from International Financial Reporting Standards (IFRS).

- FRS 100, 101 and 102 replace UK GAAP.
- The introduction of FRS 100, 101 and 102 seeks to promote harmonisation with IFRS for UK non public listed companies.
- The IFRS outlines the content and presentation of financial statements for public listed companies.
- The IFRS has identified four underlying concepts: accruals, going concern, stable measuring unit and units of constant purchasing power.
- FRS 18 identified the bedrock principles as going concern and accruals.
- FRS 18 identified the desirable principles as prudence and consistency.

Test yourself answers

Test yourself 2.1

a) Consistency and prudence.

b) Accruals and going concern.

c) Stable measuring unit and units of constant purchasing power.

Test yourself 2.2

a) The consistency concept is based on a uniformity of accounting treatment of like items within and between accounting periods. For example, the depreciation method selected for a class of property, plant and equipment will be the same within and between accounting periods.

The use of the consistency concept prevents the subjective movement between estimation bases to distort the results of financial statements.

The consistency concept increases the usefulness of accounting information and enables comparability of financial statements. The information can be compared with similar information about the company for some other period or point in time, and with similar information about other businesses.

b) Going concern is the accounting concept that assumes that a business will continue for the foreseeable future with no intentions of closing down. Examples to reflect this are payables (outstanding creditors will be paid in the future, or receivables (outstanding monies due to the business will be collected in the future) or depreciation (the cost of property, plant and equipment will be spread over the useful life of the tangible fixed asset).

c) The conservatism concept is also known as prudence.

Test yourself 2.3

a) Objectivity.

b) Duality.

c) False – profit is recognised when it is realised.

Part two

Recording financial information

Overview

This section introduces the accounting equation that underpins the process and structure of accounting and financial statements.

The accounting system perspective continues with an examination of the outputs from business transactions. This is followed by the identification and demonstration of the books of prime entry used to record the business transactions on our journey to produce the accounting information for users to make their decisions about the organisation.

The central focus of this section is Chapter 5. This chapter provides an overview of the double-entry system upon which our accounting and financial reporting systems are built. The chapter provides students with an awareness of how to record and report cash and non-cash business transactions for purchases or sales that arise during the accounting process for a business or non-commercial organisation.

Learning outcomes

At the end of this Part, you will:

- understand the accounting equation and how to classify capital, assets and liabilities
- understand the layout of financial statements and the impact of different transactions on the accounting equation
- be able to report business transactions
- be able to record the double entry for different business transactions.

Chapter three
The accounting equation

List of topics

1. The accounting equation
2. Classifying assets and liabilities
3. The balance sheet
4. The impact of trading on the owner's investment in the business
5. The profit and loss account
6. What goes where: profit and loss account or balance sheet?

Introduction

This chapter examines how accountants attempt to record the financial position of an organisation. This is achieved by introducing the accounting equation, which summarises both the assets owned by an organisation and the sources from which those assets are obtained. The sources of the assets are explained as those coming from the owner(s) and outsiders. These sources are seen as claims on the organisation's assets or liabilities to bodies outside the organisation. The accounting equation is explained as the basis for the balance sheet. This chapter examines the profit and loss account, and concludes with the recognition of what transactions are recorded in the two financial statements.

1. The accounting equation

In Chapter 1, accounting was defined as being concerned with identifying, collecting, measuring, recording, summarising and communicating the financial aspects of an organisation's activities. In order to achieve this, accountants need to have a system that will methodically collect the financial aspects of such activities. The system they use is based on the accounting equation and its expanded five elements; owner's capital, liability, assets, revenue and expenses. The first three elements form the traditional accounting equation and that is reflected in the balance sheet (statement of financial position) of any entity. The final two elements, revenue and expenses are the twin features of an entity's profit and loss account (statement of financial performance).

These five elements are examined throughout the chapter with reference to a business that is owned and set up by one person. This type of business is referred to as a sole trader, but the principles of the accounting equation demonstrated here are and can be applied to any business organisation.

owner's capital
The total of the original capital invested by the owner in the business, plus any retained profits or reserves from previous years, plus this year's profits less any drawings made by the owner during the year.

liability
The financial obligations of a business, e.g. creditors, bank and overdrafts.

The owner, Chris Black, started a business selling computers on 1 January 20X4. Black opened a business bank account and paid in £100,000. This money is termed the **owner's capital** (see below). This one action has brought into existence the financial position of the business. This can be depicted as follows in the form of an accounting equation:

Claims on assets = Assets

Total liabilities = Total assets

Owner's capital (£100,000) = Bank account (£100,000)

To represent the owner's capital as a liability may be difficult to understand. A **liability** represents a sum owed by the business to another party. If this is the case, how can the owner's investments in the business be seen as a liability? You will recall that Chapter 2 introduced the idea of the business entity concept, which means that a business is seen as a separate entity, distinct from its owners or managers. Under this concept, any monies put into a business by the owner can be regarded as a liability of the business. In simple terms, the monies put in by Chris Black have not been given to the business. From an accounting perspective, the £100,000 has been loaned to the business. Chris Black may withdraw the £100,000 at any time, provided there is sufficient cash at the bank. In effect, the business has a liability because, as a separate entity, it owes the owner £100,000.

The assets of the business represent the economic resources of the business. In this case, the assets are represented in the form of cash at the bank. The initial capital of the business records what the owner has contributed to the business from their private resources to start the business. In the above example, this is represented by cash at the bank, but the capital could be in the form of a workshop or a vehicle that the owner has 'given' to the business. The value of the workshop or vehicle represents the capital that the business owes the owner.

The accounting equation has the following important characteristics:

- The value of the assets is the same as the value of the liabilities.
- Both sides of the equation are of equal value, i.e. they balance.
- The assets of a business must come from somewhere; in fact, they are financed by the liabilities of the business – in this case, the owner's investment.
- The application of the business entity concept distinguishes the owner and the business, and thus the business incurs a liability back to the owner of the invested capital.

Test yourself 3.1

a) **The accounting equation is represented by which one of the following?**

A Assets = Capital – Liabilities

B Assets = Liabilities – Capital

C Assets + Liabilities = Capital

D Assets = Capital + Liabilities

b) **A sum of £10,000 owed by a business to another party is known as which one of the following?**

A Cash

B Assets

C Liability

D Capital

c) **The accounting equation reflects which one of the following statements?**

A The value of the assets equals the value of the liabilities.

B The value of the assets is greater than the value of the liabilities.

C The value of the assets is less than the value of the liabilities.

D The value of the assets equals the value of the capital.

The accounting equation as developed above expresses the business in terms of:

Claims on assets = Assets

or:

Total capital + Total liabilities = Total assets

Chris Black may decide that his business requires more monies and so will borrow a further £150,000 from the bank. This bank loan is a liability of the business, but at the same time the asset has increased by £150,000. The financial position of the business can now be represented in the accounting equation as follows:

Total capital	+	Total liabilities	=	Total assets
£100,000 (owner)	+	£150,000 (debt)	=	£250,000 (bank)

You can see that there are two claims on the £250,000 of assets of the business. These are Chris Black's initial start-up capital of £100,000 and the bank's claim for the £150,000 loan.

The impact of any further business transactions on the financial position of the company can be reflected in the accounting equation. Chris Black carried out the following transactions during the first week of trading. He:

1. purchased a motor vehicle for £15,000, paying by cheque;
2. withdrew £1,000 from the bank for use as a cash float; and
3. purchased shop premises for £60,000, paying by cheque.

The impact on the accounting equation of these two transactions will be as shown in Worked example 3.1.

Worked example 3.1

Transaction 1
£100,000 (owner) + £150,000 (debt) = £235,000 (bank) + £15,000 (vehicle)
£100,000 (owner) + £150,000 (liabilities) = £250,000 (assets)

Transaction 2
£100,000 (owner) + £150,000 (debt) = £234,000 (bank) + £15,000 (vehicle) + £1,000 (cash)
£100,000 (owner) + £150,000 (liabilities) = £250,000 (assets)

Transaction 3
£100,000 (owner) + £150,000 (debt) = £174,000 (bank) + £60,000 (premises) + £15,000 (vehicle) + £1,000 (cash)
£100,000 (owner) + £150,000 (liabilities) = £250,000 (assets)

Note that following all these transactions, the accounting equation is still in balance.

Recording both aspects of a transaction keeps the accounting equation in balance and is the principle underlying bookkeeping systems. Although non-accountants need not concern themselves with the mechanics of double-entry bookkeeping, it is important to appreciate that the accounting equation not only forms the basis of the balance sheet, but forms the foundation of the profit and loss account.

Test yourself 3.2

Show the accounting equation position following each of the following transactions:

a) started a business by putting £50,000 into a business bank account;

b) purchased a building for £10,000; and

c) raised a bank loan of £20,000.

2. Classifying assets and liabilities

As a business grows, it is likely to increase the number of transactions that will impact upon the value and structure of the capital, liabilities and assets, as represented in the accounting equation. Given that the equation forms the basis of the balance sheet, it will be beneficial for the users if the capital, assets and liabilities are classified. Classification means putting them into groups because they have common characteristics.

The balance sheet takes the following accounting equation already described:

Total capital + Total liabilities = Total assets

2.1 Capital

The initial cash put in by the owner is called the **capital**. Capital is a liability of the business to the owner. The size and value of this initial capital may increase over the life of the business. The capital can increase in at least two ways.

capital
The funds used by an entity for its operations.

1. The owner can put more of their own money into the business. The new funds increase the capital of the business.
2. The business itself can generate additional capital by selling goods or services at a profit. This profit is earned on behalf of the owner by the business. The profit belongs to the owner and, provided it is not taken out of the business by the owner, will increase the capital element of the accounting equation. These profits are sometimes called **retained profits**.

retained profits
Non-distributed profits retained as revenue reserve. In a not-for-profit entity, these are described as accumulated funds.

2.2 Liabilities

Liabilities are the debts of the business. They represent what the business owes to external parties other than the owner. The external liabilities or obligations, called the **creditors** of a business, may be classified according to the time period within which they have to be settled. Thus there are:

creditors
Persons or businesses to whom money is owed.

- **long-term liabilities**, which include bank loans which normally do not fall due for repayment within one year. These long-term liabilities are also called 'creditors: amounts falling due after more than one year'; and
- **current liabilities** or 'creditors: amounts falling due within one year'. These are liabilities that will fall due for repayment within one year. An example is monies owed to suppliers for goods bought on credit and that are not paid for until some time after they have been delivered. These types of current liability are also called trade creditors. Other examples of current liabilities include bank overdrafts and taxes owed to the government, both of which have to be settled within 12 months.

long-term liabilities
Persons or businesses to whom money is owed and the debt is payable beyond 12 months.

current liabilities
Persons or businesses to whom money is owed and falls due and payable within 12 months.

2.3 Assets

An asset is something with a value which a business owns or has the use of, e.g. factories, office buildings, warehouses, delivery vans, lorries, plant and machinery. Assets also include such things as computer equipment, office furniture and cash, as well as stock or inventory held in store awaiting sale to customers. The term can also be used to cover raw materials and components held in store by a manufacturing business for use in production. They provide a benefit to the firm.

Assets can be divided into two broad categories: fixed assets and current assets.

1. *Fixed assets*

fixed assets
Assets owned by an entity with a lifespan greater than 12 months.

Fixed assets are assets that are bought and expected to be used within the business for several years. Fixed assets are not bought with the intention of being resold/converted. Fixed assets are permanent and give long-term benefits to the business, which is why they are termed fixed. Fixed assets may be subdivided into three types: tangible, intangible and investments.

tangible fixed assets
A group of fixed assets owned by an entity with a lifespan greater than 12 months with a physical existence.

intangible fixed assets
A group of fixed assets owned by an entity with a lifespan greater than 12 months that do not have a physical existence; they cannot be seen or touched.

- **Tangible fixed assets**: Factories, office buildings and warehouses are clearly tangible and so are delivery vans, lorries and cars, even though they can move about; these are tangible fixed assets.
- **Intangible fixed assets**: Not all assets have a physical form like those described above; some are intangible. Intangible fixed assets are useful not because of their physical characteristics but because the rights they carry can be extremely valuable. Two principal examples are patents and trademarks.

  Patents are where the government grants a patent owner the exclusive right for a period of years to produce and sell a particular invention, such as a mini music system. Trademarks or brand names are the distinctive identifications by which customers recognise a product or service – for example, the logos of Nike, Coca-Cola or Apple Computers. These are intangible assets.
- **Investments**: This is where one company invests into another company. The investing company expects to hold its investment for over 12 months. The investment provides the investing company with an income in the form of interest or dividends.

2. *Current assets*

current assets
Assets that will change their form in a short period of time.

debtors
Persons or businesses who owe money to a business.

Current assets are those assets that, within a short period of time, will change their form. These assets will be converted into cash within a year in the normal course of trading. The form of current assets is constantly changing. Examples of current assets include stock, **debtors**, bank and cash balances.

This classification allows us to amend the accounting equation from its original format:

Total capital + Total liabilities = Total assets

to:

Total capital = Total assets – Total liabilities

or:

Capital = Fixed assets + Current assets – Current liabilities – Long-term liabilities

£100,000	=	£60,000	+	£15,000	+	£174,000	+	£1,000	–	£150,000
(owner)		(premises)		(vehicle)		(bank)		(cash)		(debt)
£100,000	=	[£60,000 + £15,000]			+	[£174,000 + £1,000]			–	£150,000
		£100,000 = £75,000			+	£175,000 – £150,000				

£100,000 = £250,000 – £150,000

£100,000 = £100,000

Test yourself 3.3

a) A factory is an example of which one of the following?

A Current asset

B Current liability

C Tangible fixed asset

D Intangible fixed asset

b) A patent is an example of which one of the following?

A Current asset

B Current liability

C Tangible fixed asset

D Intangible fixed asset

c) A bank overdraft is an example of which one of the following?

A Current asset

B Current liability

C Tangible fixed asset

D Intangible fixed asset

3. The balance sheet

The balance sheet is a development of the accounting equation. The balance sheet has the primary purpose of reporting the financial position of an organisation at a single point in time.

The financial position is shown as follows:

Fixed assets + Current assets – Current liabilities – Long-term liabilities = Initial capital + Retained profits

If we refer to the accounting equation created earlier, we can create a very simple balance sheet as follows.

Worked example 3.2

Balance sheet of Chris Black as at end of week 1

Fixed assets	**£**	**£**
Premises		60,000
Vehicles		15,000
		75,000
Current assets		
Bank	174,000	
Cash	1,000	175,000
		250,000
Less current liabilities		nil
Less long-term liabilities		
Bank loan		150,000
		100,000
Initial capital		100,000
Plus retained profits		nil
		100,000

The title of the balance sheet includes the business name, Chris Black, and is stated at a point in time: 'as at'. The balance sheet is a position statement or 'snapshot' of the business's assets and the claims on those assets at a point in time.

The balance sheet format starts to group certain items together, for example, the bank and cash as current assets.

Certain figures are added to produce subtotals and totals – for example, the fixed assets, premises and vehicles are added together to give a figure for total fixed assets.

Grouping similar items and providing subtotals are intended to assist the users of balance sheets.

The business, which is only just beginning, has not yet incurred any current liabilities such as creditors or overdrafts.

Most importantly, the business has not yet generated any profits, so there are no retained profits.

4. The impact of trading on the owner's investment in the business

So far the accounting equation recording the financial position of Chris Black has not involved buying or selling goods or incurring any expenses. These are essential activities if the business is to grow by selling its goods at profit.

Chris Black buys and sells computers. Computers are the goods the business buys with the intention of reselling. These are called stocks. In order to start, Chris Black decides in week 2 of trading to purchase £50,000 of computers on credit. This activity does not generate any profit as the transaction is only increasing the current asset stock and creating a creditor, or current liability, of £50,000. The revised balance sheet appears as shown in Worked example 3.3.

Worked example 3.3

Balance sheet of Chris Black as at end of week 2

	£	£	£
Fixed assets			
Premises			60,000
Vehicles			15,000
			75,000
Current assets			
Stock	50,000		
Bank	174,000		
Cash	1,000	225,000	
Less current liabilities			
Trade creditors		50,000	
Working capital			175,000
			250,000
Less long-term liabilities			
Bank loan			150,000
			100,000
Initial capital			100,000
Plus retained profits			nil
			100,000

working capital
The capital available for conducting the day-to-day operations of an organisation; normally the excess of current assets over current liabilities.

The balance sheet shows at the end of week Chris Black has **working capital** of £175,000. Working capital is also known as net current assets and is sometimes abbreviated as WC or NCA in financial reports. Working capital is the difference between the current assets and current liabilities. Working capital is examined further in Chapter 11.

During the third week of trading, Chris Black's computers, which cost £10,000, were sold for £14,000. The customers all paid by cheque, and the cheques were banked on the same day. It is apparent that the sale of the computers has generated a profit of £4,000 – the difference between the cost price and the selling price. How will this impact on Chris Black's investment in the business, and in turn how will this affect the accounting equation and the balance sheet?

We saw in Chapter 2 that accountants calculate profit (or loss) by applying the accruals concept. This concept states that when computing profit, the sales income (or sales revenue) earned should be matched only against the expenditure incurred when earning it. In this case:

$$\text{Sales revenue} - \text{Expenses} = \text{Profit}$$
$$£14{,}000 - £10{,}000 = £4{,}000$$

The business has generated a profit on behalf of Chris Black and is owed to Chris Black by the business. Recording this liability of the business to Chris Black is shown on the liabilities side of the equation, specifically the capital and retained profits section. The profits earned are in effect additional capital reinvested by Chris Black and are called retained profits.

The sale of the computers that cost £10,000 has reduced the current asset stock by that amount. The proceeds of the sale have been banked, so the current asset at the bank has increased by £14,000. It is apparent that the accounting equation and balance sheet will not balance, as the adjustments made are not of equal value. In order to correct these imbalances, we need to record the £4,000 on the liabilities side of the equation, specifically in the capital and retained profits section. In effect, the value of Chris Black's investment in the business has grown by £4,000. The impact of the sale of the computers and the profit it creates on both the accounting equation and the balance sheet is shown below:

$$\text{Total capital} = \text{Total assets} - \text{Total liabilities}$$

Or, allowing for the profit generated:

$$\text{Capital} + (\text{Revenues} - \text{Expenses}) = \text{Fixed assets} + (\text{Current assets} - \text{Current liabilities}) - \text{Long-term liabilities}$$

$$£100{,}000 + (£14{,}000 - £10{,}000) = £75{,}000 + (£229{,}000 - £50{,}000) - £150{,}000$$

$$£104{,}000 = £104{,}000$$

Worked example 3.4

Balance sheet of Chris Black as at end of week 3

	£	£	£
Fixed assets			
Premises			60,000
Vehicles			15,000
			75,000
Current assets			
Stock (– 10,000)	40,000		
Bank (+ 14,000)	188,000		
Cash	1,000	229,000	
Less current liabilities			
Trade creditors		50,000	179,000
Working capital			254,000
Less long-term liabilities			
Bank loan			150,000
			104,000
Initial capital			100,000
Plus retained profits (+ 4000)			4,000
			104,000

Points to note:

1. The sale of stock for cheque reduces the stock balance and increases the bank balance.
2. The sale of stock at a selling price greater than cost price will generate a profit.
3. The profit increases the owner's investments in the business by increasing the retained profits.

During the fourth week of trading, the following activities take place.

1. Chris sells computers costing £6,000 for £11,000, but the customer was granted 30 days' credit.
2. Chris also paid wages of £500 by cheque.

Obviously the value of the stock goes down by £6,000 and a profit of £5,000 is made on the sale of the computers. However, the customer owes the business £11,000, so the current asset, debtors, is increased by this amount.

Similarly, the payment of wages is an expense and will reduce the profits for the period by £500. The current asset, bank balance, will be reduced by the £500 payment.

In summary:

1. Sales revenue – expenses = profit. In this example £11,000 (revenue) – (£6,000 (stock) + £500 (wages)) = £4,500 retained profits.
2. Stock reduced by £6,000 and debtors increased by £11,000.
3. Bank balance reduced by £500.

Chris Black's investment in the business has grown in week 4 by a further £4,500. Total profits for the first month's trading amount to £8,500 (week 3 (£4,000) + week 4 (£4,500)).

Worked example 3.5

Balance sheet of Chris Black as at the end of week 4

	£	£	£
Fixed assets			
Premises			60,000
Vehicles			15,000
			75,000
Current assets			
Debtors (+ 11,000)	11,000		
Stock (– 6,000)	34,000		
Bank (– 500)	187,500		
Cash	1,000	233,500	
Less current liabilities			
Trade creditors		50,000	183,500
Working capital			258,500
Less long-term liabilities			
Bank loan			150,000
			108,500
Initial capital			100,000
Plus retained profits (+ 4,500)			8,500
			108,500

Points to note:

1. The sale of stock reduces the current asset, stock, and increases the expenses by the cost price of the stock that is sold. The selling price of the stock increases the revenue for the period.
2. The sale is on credit, so there is an increase in trade debtors by the selling price of the stock.

Test yourself 3.4

Complete the missing entries labelled A–F in the following balance sheets.

Year ended 31 July	Fixed asset	Current assets	Current liabilities	Working capital	Long-term liabilities	Net assets
Year 1	12,154	7,048	A	486	B	695
Year 2	C	9,058	3,825	D	6,089	1,528
Year 3	2,154	E	8,752	1,185	5,572	F

5. The profit and loss account

The transactions of Chris Black during January 20X4 are summarised in the profit and loss account. This document shows how the business has generated profits/sustained losses over a specified period. It is a period statement as described in its title: 'Profit and loss account for year ending 20X4'.

The calculation of profit involves identifying the sales revenue of a business and comparing this with the expenditure incurred in generating that income. A typical profit and loss account for the first month's trading, based on the information provided about Chris Black's business, is shown in Worked example 3.6.

Worked example 3.6

Chris Black

Profit and loss account for the month ending 31 January 200X

	£	£
Sales		25,000
Opening stock	nil	
Add purchases	50,000	
	50,000	
Less closing stock	34,000	
Cost of goods sold		16,000
Gross profit		9,000
Less expenses		
Wages	500	
Sub total		500
Net profit		8,500

Points to note:

1. Sale is the value of the goods sold, or services performed – say in a hairdressing salon or an accounting practice. If a business sells goods on credit, it counts as sales the value of goods dispatched or services performed during the period, not just the cash the business has received.

gross profit
Sales less the cost of goods sold.

2. It is usual to identify **gross profit** – that is, sales revenue less the cost of goods sold. Gross profit results from matching the revenue earned and the expenditure incurred in providing the goods or services, which is called the cost of goods sold.

Cost of goods sold or cost of sales is calculated as follows:

	£	£
Opening stock	O	
Add purchases	P	
		O + P
Less closing stock		C
Cost of goods sold		O + P – C

This calculation is inset in the left-hand column between sales and **cost of sales**.

- The stock figures are the value of goods held for sale to customers at the beginning (opening stock) or end (closing stock) of the accounting period.
- **Purchases** are the value of goods received in the accounting period. This does not equal the cash paid to creditors.
- **Expenses** are the expenses of operating the business for the accounting period. In the case of Chris Black, the one expense is wages and the cost included is the same as the cash paid out. But there will be other bills such as telephone, rent, rates and insurance where the cost for the period is unlikely to be the same as those bills that have been paid. Refer back to the accruals concept as described in Chapter 2.
- A profit and loss account matches the revenue earned in a period with the costs incurred in earning it.
- **Net profit** is gross profit minus expenses. Remember that a business can incur a net loss if its sales revenue is less than its expenses. Net profits will increase an owner's capital while a net loss will reduce the owner's capital.

cost of sales
The sum of variable cost of sales plus factory overhead attributable to the turnover. It may also be referred to as production cost of sales or cost of goods sold.

purchases
Raw materials purchased for incorporation into products or finished goods purchased for resale.

expenses
The expenses of operating the business for the accounting period.

net profit
Gross profit less operational expenses.

Test yourself 3.5

Calculate the value of each of the missing items labelled A–F in the following.

Year ending 31 January	Turnover	Opening stock	Purchases	Closing stock	Cost of sales	Gross profit
Year 1	102,600	A	20,475	26,910	B	69,848
Year 2	108,000	35,625	C	22,425	29,580	D
Year 3	E	28,500	12,600	F	21,600	68,400

6. What goes where: profit and loss account or balance sheet?

Students need to be able to show the impact of business transactions on the balance sheet and profit and loss account. In order to assist business managers in recognising how their actions and the actions of their colleagues impact on the balance sheet and profit and loss account, Table 3.1 shows the transactions of Chris Black during January 20X4. The table summarises the impact of the transactions in the accounting equation and identifies which of the financial statements each transaction is recorded in.

Table 3.1: What goes where: balance sheet or profit and loss account

Transaction	Impact on accounting equation	Recorded in
Opened a business bank account and paid in £100,000.	Increases current asset, bank and increases owner's capital.	Balance sheet
Purchased a motor vehicle for £15,000 paying by cheque.	Increases fixed asset, vehicles and decreases current assets, bank.	Balance sheet
Withdrew £1,000 from the bank for use as cash float.	Decreases current asset, bank and increases current asset, cash.	Balance sheet
Purchased shop premises for £60,000 paying by cheque.	Increases fixed asset, premises and decreases current assets, bank.	Balance sheet
Purchased £50,000 of computers on credit.	Increases current asset, stock and increases current liability, trade creditors.	Balance sheet
Computers costing £10,000 are sold for £14,000. The customers all pay by cheque which is banked on the same day.	Decreases current asset, stock and increases current asset, bank. Increases revenue and increases expenses.	Balance sheet and profit and loss account
Computers costing £6,000 are sold for £11,000 but the customer is granted 30 days' credit.	Decreases current asset, stock and increases current asset, debtors. Increases revenue and increases expenses.	Balance sheet and profit and loss account
Paid wages by cheque of £500.	Increases expenses and decreases current asset, bank.	Balance sheet and profit and loss account

It is important to understand the distinction between balance sheet items and profit and loss account items. A useful way of looking at it is to identify whether a payment has been for consumable items (expenses such as salaries, heating, lighting, bank interest, etc.), which are unlikely to be present at the year-end. These are all profit and loss items. Alternatively, payments may be for longer-term items (purchase of assets), which are all balance sheet items. These are likely to be there at the year-end.

Resources added to the business can come from the owner (capital), outside lenders (long-term loans) or traders granting credit (creditors). These are all balance sheet items.

One point to note is that the purchase of stock involves payments which initially increase the asset stock and so are reflected in the balance sheet. However, when the stock is sold, it turns into an expense and is shown in the profit and loss account through the cost of goods sold calculation.

Accounting systems will record the payment of invoices to suppliers of goods or services. A decision has to be made as to whether the bills received are recorded as an asset or an expense. This depends on whether the benefit of the goods or service being charged has been partly or fully received in the accounting period. For example, a business may purchase items of stock for resale. However, at the balance sheet date, some of the stock items may remain unsold; the benefit from this unsold stock has not been received and so the closing stock is deducted from the expenditure related to the accounting period and is shown on the balance sheet as a current asset. The stock is charged, or 'expensed', in the period in which it is consumed.

Chapter summary

- The accounting equation is central to the study of accounting fundamentals.
- The accounting equation (total assets = total liabilities + total capital) is a reflection of the balance sheet.
- Total assets should always equal total liabilities.
- When recording a transaction, it is important to remember to balance both sides of the equation. This is the principle behind double-entry bookkeeping.
- 'Asset' is a general term for the resources in any organisation.
- Assets are classified as fixed assets or non-current assets, and current assets.
- Fixed assets or non-current assets are items purchased by an organisation to provide economic benefits and have an economic lifespan beyond 12 months.
- Current assets are items that can be converted into cash during the normal course of trading, such as stock and debtors.
- Liabilities are the external debts of an organisation, and they are classified as long-term liabilities (non-current liabilities) and current liabilities.
- Long-term liabilities (non-current liabilities) are obligations that do not fall due for repayment within one year.
- Current liabilities are obligations due for payment within a year.
- The balance sheet reports the financial position of the organisation at a point in time.
- The profit and loss account provides a summary of the annual performance of an organisation measured in terms of profit.

Test yourself answers

Test yourself 3.1

a) D – Assets = Capital + Liabilities
b) C – Liability
c) A – The value of the assets equals the value of the liabilities.

Test yourself 3.2

Total capital + Total liabilities = Total assets

a) Total capital + Total Liabilities = Bank + Fixed assets
50,000 + 0 = 50,000
50,000 = 50,000

b) Total capital + Total liabilities = Bank + Building
50,000 + 0 = 40,000 + 10,000
50,000 = 50,000

c) Total capital + Total liabilities = Bank + Building
50,000 + 20,000 = 60,000 + 10,000
70,000 = 70,000

Test yourself 3.3

a) C – Tangible fixed asset
b) D – Intangible fixed asset
c) B – Current liability

Test yourself 3.4

A 6,562
B 11,945
C 2,384
D 5,233
E 9,937
F (2,233)

Test yourself 3.5

A 39,187
B 32,752
C 16,380
D 78,420
E 90,000
F 19,500

Chapter four

Accounting system and accounting records

List of topics

1. Source documents
2. Books of prime entry
3. Cash books
4. The journal
5. Ledger accounts
6. Putting it all together

Introduction

This chapter provides a structured journey from the business transaction process to the reporting of the transactions in the accounting ledgers in preparation for the production of the annual accounts. On route to the production of the accounting ledgers, this chapter examines the different source documents from the business transaction process and moves on to identify the books of prime entry for reporting the business transaction.

The journey is completed with an examination of the system of double entry, which underpins our traditional accounting and reporting process. This is looked at in more detail in Chapter 5.

1. Source documents

Business transactions are nearly always recorded on a document. These **source documents** contain information that is fed into an accounting system to form the basis of the information in the accounts. Such documents include the following.

source documents
Documents that contain the information that is put into an accounting system.

- **Sales order**: A customer provides a written order detailing the goods or services they wish to buy.
- **Purchase order**: A business sends a written order to a supplier for the purchase of goods or materials.

- **Invoice from suppliers**: A business buys goods or services from a supplier and receives an invoice from the supplier. Note that the goods or services received should correspond to the details on the purchase order.
- **Invoice sent to customers**: A business sells goods or services to a customer and sends an invoice to the customer. The details on the invoice should correspond to the details on the sales order. An example of the content of an invoice issued by the supplier New Bizness Stationers to the customer Prophett & Loss Accountants is shown in Figure 4.1.

New Bizness Stationers
7c Churchville Towers
Old Town
OT2 6AD
Tel: 0123 246 9753
E: sales@nbizstat.com

Date: 10 Nov 20X0

Order Ref: P0237PL

Invoice No: NBS675492

To:

Prophett & Loss Accountants
1 Park View
Broad Town
BT1 2ME

Date	**Description**	**Unit price**	**Total**
5 Nov 20X0	5 dozen A4 4-ring binders	£1.50	£90.00
5 Nov 20X0	100 reams of green A4 paper	£3.99	£399.00
		Total payable	£489.00

Payment terms 30 days. 1% cash discount if invoice paid within 14 days.

Figure 4.1: Sample invoice

Other source documents include:

- credit notes from suppliers for purchases returned, or to customers for sales returned. Credit notes are sent out when goods or services are returned to the supplier by the customer. The credit note contains the same information as an invoice, but is usually printed in red. In effect, credit notes represent negative sales invoices; and
- goods received note (GRN) – these are sent with goods as they are shipped to the customer. The GRN is used to book the goods into the warehouse. A copy of the GRN is usually sent to the accounts department before an invoice can be paid.

2. Books of prime entry

In the early days of accounting, the information on the source documents was copied each day by a clerk into a book. This book is the source of any accounting entry, and gives it authority; it is called a **book of prime entry**.

book of prime entry
A first record of transactions, such as sales or purchases, from which details or totals, as appropriate, are transferred to the ledgers.

There is no such thing as a typical accounting system, as many of these books have been computerised or replaced by files of invoices which carry out the same function. However, familiarity with the purpose, use and effects of these important accounting documents will help accounting students understand how basic accounting systems work. Figure 4.2 shows what business transactions are entered into each book of prime entry.

Business transactions						
Sales	Purchases	Bank receipts or payments	Sales returns	Purchase returns	Minor cash expenses	Sundry items

↓ ↓ ↓ ↓ ↓ ↓ ↓

Books of prime entry						
Sales daybook	Purchase daybook	Cash book	Sales returns daybook	Purchase returns daybook	Petty cash book	Journal

Figure 4.2: The relationship between the business transactions and books of prime entry

Test yourself 4.1

a) **Which source document is sent with goods as they are shipped to the customer?**

   A Sales order

   B Credit note

   C Goods received note

   D Invoice from supplier

b) **Which source document is given to a customer when returning goods to a supplier?**

   A Sales order

   B Credit note

   C Goods received note

   D Invoice from supplier

c) **Explain what a source document is.**

2.1 Sales daybook

This book records all the sales invoices that a business has sent out to its customers. Every sale, both cash sales and on credit, should have an invoice raised. These invoices should be recorded in the sales daybook. Each page of the sales daybook is sequentially numbered to assist in the financial control of sales, as is each invoice.

Date	Invoice no.	Customer	Sales ledger page	Total invoiced
Feb 20X4	1311	I. Back & Co.	B104	£15,000
	1312	L. Coe Ltd	C123	£3,400

Figure 4.3: Sample sales daybook

At the end of each day, each invoice should be entered, or 'posted', to the individual customer's account in the sales ledger. This ledger contains an account for each customer and shows the business how much is owed by each of its customers, i.e. its trade debtors. The customers' accounts can be found by reference to the unique customer code.

Periodically, the total of the sales daybook page is analysed by credit sales, and the totals posted or entered to the sales account.

2.2 Sales returns daybook

Goods sold to customers are often returned for some reason such as:

- the goods are faulty; or
- the wrong goods have been supplied.

This return may be for all the sold goods, in which case the entire original invoice has to be cancelled. Alternatively, only a few of the goods are returned, in which case only part of the invoice may be offset. To achieve this, credit notes are issued. The sales returns daybook should be completed in exactly the same way as the sales daybook in respect of goods returned from customers. When the individual entries are made to the sales ledger, they will reduce the amount owed by the customer. The sales returns will also reduce the sales achieved by the business, but they are posted to a separate account labelled Sales Returns or Returns Inward.

2.3 Purchases daybook

This book contains information about the purchases made by a business and is a list of invoices from suppliers (see Figure 4.4 for an example). It is completed in exactly the same way as the sales daybook, with each page being sequentially numbered. The invoice is the source document and describes the goods and services provided, and the price the buyer has to pay. It will also contain a cross-reference to the order number issued by the business to raise the purchase.

The individual invoices will be posted to the supplier's accounts in the purchases ledger, which contains an account for each supplier. This account will record the individual invoices received from the supplier and ultimately the payments made to the supplier by the business. At any point in time the supplier's account shows the financial position between the business and the supplier.

Date	Purchases	Supplier ledger page	Total invoiced (£)
25 Feb 20X4	ABC Ltd.	A/01	3,305
26 Feb 20X4	XYZ Ltd	X12	2,809
28 Feb 20X4	RST & Co.	R/21	860

Figure 4.4: Sample purchases daybook

2.4 Purchases returns daybook

Purchases returns are goods a business returns to a supplier. In effect they are negative purchases in that they reduce the amount owed to a supplier. This will be completed in exactly the same manner as the purchase daybook. When the entries are made to the purchases ledger, they will reduce the amounts owing to the suppliers and will reduce the purchases made by the business.

2.5 Reasons to maintain separate returns daybooks

The return of goods to a supplier would suggest a deduction is made from the purchases account to reflect the return of the goods. Similarly, the supplier should make a reduction in their sales account to reflect the return of the previously sold item.

However, the recording of purchase and sales returns is not a simple exercise of deducting the total of the return goods from the previously purchased or sold totals. A separate purchase and sales return account must be opened, as explained above.

The separation of the returns from the purchases and sales provides business owners with the full knowledge of their actual sales, purchases and returned items. The level or volume of returns may be indicative of a problem in the production or distribution process. It is for this reason that the purchase returns are not deducted from the purchases in the purchase daybook and similarly for the sales return. The accounting for the purchases and sales is part of an information system to allow the users to make decisions and not a mathematical exercise of additions and subtractions.

Worked example 4.1

In January 20X4, the company Gingico returned four items to their original suppliers and they received the following credit notes from the suppliers:

12 January 20X4: credit note 9012 returns to Poshco, £21,876

19 January 20X4: credit note 9013 returns to Babyco, £31,972

26 January 20X4: credit note 9014 returns to Sportico, £9,341

30 January 20X4: credit note 9015 returns to Fiestico, £15,332

Prepare Gingico's purchase returns daybook for the month of January 20XX.

Answer

Purchase returns daybook			
Date	**Credit note no.**	**Supplier**	**Amount £**
9 Jan 20X4	9012	Poshco	21,876
12 Jan 20X4	9013	Babyco	31,972
26 Jan 20X4	9014	Sportico	9,341
30 Jan 20X4	9015	Fiestico	15,332
Transfer to purchase returns account			78,521

The balance from the purchase returns daybook is transferred to the purchase returns account in the general ledger.

Test yourself 4.2

a) **In which book of prime entry would a transaction reduce the sales of a business?**

A Sales daybook

B Purchases daybook

C Sales return daybook

D Purchases return daybook

b) New Bizness Stationers has recently received an invoice from one of its suppliers. In which book of prime entry should their bookkeeper record the invoice received?

A Sales daybook

B Purchases daybook

C Sales return daybook

D Purchases return daybook

3. Cash books

For accounting purposes, 'cash' includes cash, cheques and bank transactions, unless specified as 'cash in hand' or 'petty cash' (see below). The **cash book** records all 'cash' transactions including coins, banknotes, cheques, direct debits, credit transfers and banker's drafts. The cash book is split into columns for cash and bank transactions.

cash book
A book that records the cash accounts of a business.

The cash book has one page for receipts from customers, depending on whether it is in the form of cash or cheque. On the opposite side of the cash book will be a page for payments to creditors and for other expenses such as wages, electricity, etc.

Worked example 4.2

The cash book of Becco showed an overdraft balance of £745 on 30 November 20X4. The following transactions took place in December 20X4:

3 Dec 20X4: Received £3,000 loan from bank.

7 Dec 20X4: Sold goods to A. Dye on credit for £11,750.

8 Dec 20X4: Paid £2,500 for this quarter's rent.

12 Dec 20X4: Paid insurance £1,670.

16 Dec 20X4: Bank agreed an overdraft of £10,000.

19 Dec 20X4: Received £6,450 from Mex Ltd.

Prepare Becco's cash book for the month of December 20X4.

Answer

Becco cash book				
Date	**Details**	**Receipts £**	**Payments £**	**Balance £**
30 Nov 20X4	Balance b/d			(745)
3 Dec 20X4	Loan	3,000		2,255
8 Dec 20X4	Rent		2,500	(245)
12 Dec 20X4	Insurance		1,670	(1,915)

29 Dec 20X4	Mex Ltd	6,450		4,535
31 Dec 20X4	Balance c/d			4,535

Two important points should be noted when answering this question and all questions regarding the cash book: firstly, the status of the opening balance and secondly, the fact that the cash book only records actual cash movements (receipts and payments).

The opening balance is overdrawn, so the opening balance of £745 is expressed as a negative or in brackets to denote a negative. Secondly, two items supplied do not involve any cash movement. The sale of goods on 7 December is a credit sale which means the buyer, A. Dye, will pay at a later date. When they make their payment is when a cash inflow will be recorded. The bank's agreement to an overdraft on 16 December does not involve any cash movement. The bank has granted the company the facility to go overdrawn up to £10,000. It does not involve a transfer of £10,000 into the bank account.

An alternative method to derive the closing balance would be as follows:

	£
Opening balance	O
Plus receipts in period	R
Less payments in period	(P)
Balance at the end of the period	O + R – P

However, this format would not answer the question in an examination because it does not show the cash book for the month. This approach only provides the opening and closing balances. Although mathematically correct, the alternative approach does not provide the correct answer required.

For information purposes, the alternative method using the facts from the question is shown below and shows the correct opening and closing balances. It does not provide any information of the cash book movement throughout the month.

		£
30 Nov 20X4	Balance b/d	(745)
	December receipts	9,450
	December payments	(4,170)
	Balance at 31 December 20X4	4,535

petty cash account
A record of relatively small cash receipts and payments, the balance representing the cash in the control of an individual, usually dealt with under an imprest system.

3.1 Petty cash book

Sometimes an organisation, regardless of its size, finds itself in a situation where it has to make or reimburse small-value payments. Such payments may be for stamps, taxi fares, tea or coffee for the office, or emergency purchases of stationery. Most businesses keep a small amount of cash on their premises for this purpose. This cash or float is called a **petty cash account**. As the cash used to finance the petty cash float is normally transferred from the bank account, it is in effect a subsidiary of the main cash book. Petty cash payments and receipts are recorded in a **petty cash book**. The petty cash is usually the responsibility of the petty cashier.

petty cash book
A book for recording receipts and payments made out of a petty cash account.

A common way of maintaining petty cash is by using the **imprest system**. A fixed float is given to the petty cashier. When a purchase is made, a petty cash voucher is completed and filed, together with the proof of purchase, such as a receipt. At any one time the balance of the petty cash plus the total of all the petty cash vouchers should equal the amount of the original cash float. This method acts as an automatic internal check on the accuracy and honesty of the cashier. When the petty cashier needs to replenish the float, they present the vouchers to the main cashier, who then reimburses the petty cashier with cash equal to the value of the vouchers. The petty cash vouchers are then entered in the expense accounts of the main accounting system.

imprest system
A method of controlling cash or stock; when the cash or stock has been reduced by disbursements or issues, it is restored to its original level.

Worked example 4.3

Company ABC had a petty cash balance of £2,000 at 30 November 20X4. Petty cash experience in the month ended 31 December 20X4 was £890. The petty cash imprest is to be increased to £2,500 at 31 December 20X4.

How much cash must company ABC withdraw from the bank to have the correct imprest at 31 December 20X4?

Answer

Petty cash	**£**
Balance at 30 November 20X4	2,000
Expenditure in December 20X4	890
	1,110
Required bank balance	
At 31 December 20X4	2,500
Balance to be withdrawn from bank	1,390

A bank withdrawal of £1,139 will be required to restore the petty cash imprest to £2,500

4. The journal

The **journal** is used to make entries in the ledger that cannot be made through the other books of prime entry. Examples are the correction of posting errors in the ledger or the formal entry of accounting adjustments, such as depreciation and accruals, at the end of the year, correction of errors and large or unusual transactions.

journal
A record of financial transactions, such as transfers between accounts, not dealt with elsewhere.

Test yourself 4.3

a) Explain the term 'cash' as used in cash book.

b) Explain why organisations keep a petty cash book and a cash book.

5. Ledger accounts

The ledger is a book that consists of pages called accounts. There is an account in the ledger for each different type of item the business wishes to analyse. The accounts can be either:

- personal accounts of the customers (debtors) which are kept in the **sales or debtors ledger**. Personal accounts of suppliers (creditors) which are kept in the **purchases or creditors ledger**; or
- impersonal accounts, which includes accounts such as sales, purchases, wages, depreciation, stocks, cash and bank, fixed assets, capital and liabilities, etc. It will also include the total debtors and total creditors of the business. These accounts are kept in the **nominal ledger**.

sales or debtors ledger
A collection of the accounts or records receivable from each customer.

purchases or creditors ledger
A ledger for a supplier's personal account.

nominal ledger
A ledger for impersonal accounts.

5.1 Sales or debtors ledger

The sales ledger contains an account or record for each customer. Invoices raised will be posted to the account to increase the customer's indebtedness, while credit notes will be posted to reduce their indebtedness. Any cash received will be posted to the cash book and to the customer's account to reduce their indebtedness. The balance column on the account shows at any one time how much is owing by that customer.

5.2 Purchases or creditors ledger

This will be completed in a similar manner to the sales ledger. This ledger contains an account or record for each supplier. Invoices received will be posted to the account to increase the amount owed to the supplier, while the credit notes will be posted to reduce the business's indebtedness. Any cash paid will be posted to the cash book and to the suppliers account to reduce the business's indebtedness. The balance column on the account shows at any one time how much is owed by the business to that supplier.

5.3 Nominal (or general) ledger

This ledger is made up of all the non-personal accounts – in contrast to the personal ledgers, which include the names of customers and suppliers.

Examples of accounts in the nominal ledger include:

- fixed assets at cost – a separate account for each type of fixed asset, e.g. motor vehicles, machinery;

- provision for depreciation of fixed assets – a separate account for each provision, e.g. provision for depreciation of motor vehicles, provision for depreciation of motor vehicles;
- capital account – of owner;
- stocks of finished goods;
- total debtors;
- total creditors;
- expense accounts – a separate account for each expense, e.g. salaries, heating, bank charges, petrol;
- sales income; and
- total cash.

These accounts form the basis for preparing the profit and loss account and balance sheet.

Test yourself 4.4

a) **Outline the difference between personal accounts and impersonal accounts.**

b) **Outline the contents of a sales ledger.**

6. Putting it all together

The previous sections of this chapter have described how accounting entries are recorded from the source documents to the books of prime entry to the individual accounts in the accounting books or ledger. This can be quite daunting for students as there is a lot of terminology, complicated by the fact that many of the terms have alternative names. Figure 4.5 provides clarification of the process. The following chapter will focus on the application of **double entry** to record the business transactions.

double entry
A method of recording transactions in ledger accounts so that the monetary value of the debits and credits always balance each other.

Business transactions						
Sales	Purchases	Bank receipts or payments	Sales returns	Purchase returns	Minor cash expenses	Sundry items

Books of prime entry						
Sales daybook	Purchase daybook	Cash book	Sales returns daybook	Purchase returns daybook	Petty cash book	Journal

Ledger accounts		
Purchases (creditors) ledger. This ledger contains an account or record for each supplier.	Nominal ledger or general ledger. This ledger includes accounts such as sales, purchases, wages, depreciation, stocks, cash, bank, debtors, creditors and fixed assets.	Sales (debtors) ledger. This ledger contains an account or record for each customer.

Books of prime entry	
Income and expenses accounts = The profit and loss account = Income statement = Statement of comprehensive income	Assets, capital and liabilities = The balance sheet = Statement of financial position

Figure 4.5: The journey from business transactions to financial statements

Chapter summary

- Business transactions are nearly always recorded on documents that are the source of the information in the accounts.
- The information is copied from source documents into books of prime entry.
- The books of prime entry perform the key roles of not only being the source of all accounting entries but also giving authority to those entries.
- The books of prime entry are linked to recording business transactions.
- The sales daybook records all the sales invoices that a business has sent out to its customers.
- Goods returned by the customer are recorded in the sales returns daybook.
- The purchases daybook contains information about the purchases made by an organisation while the goods returned back to a supplier are recorded in the purchase returns daybook.
- The cash book records cash movements in and out of the business.
- For accounting purposes, cash includes cheques and bank transactions, coins, banknotes, cheques, direct debits, credit transfers and banker's drafts.
- The petty cash book is a book for recording small value payments. The journal is the book used to make entries into the ledger that cannot be made through the other books of prime entry.

Test yourself answers

Test yourself 4.1

a) C – Goods received note

b) B – Credit note

c) A source document is any document that a business must retain from any business transaction containing information used as an input into the accounting system.

Test yourself 4.2

a) C – Sales return daybook

b) B – Purchases daybook

Test yourself 4.3

a) The term refers to cash and cash equivalents such as cheque or bank transactions. These transactions are all recorded in the cash book.

b) A cash book is used to record all the cash transactions of an organisation. A petty cash book is used to record only the minor or smaller operational cash transactions of an organisation, such as stamps or milk for the office, or a taxi.

Test yourself 4.4

a) Personal accounts are the accounts of the individual or entity with which a business or organisation conducts business, such as Ms Jones or Dr Blue. Impersonal accounts are the accounts for the nature of the business transaction such as sales, administration or capital. The personal accounts in aggregate are maintained in a purchases or creditors ledger account. For example, all purchases from Dr Blue will be found in the purchases ledger account.

b) A sales ledger holds an account or record for each customer. Invoices raised will be posted to the account to increase the customer's indebtedness, while credit notes will be posted to reduce their indebtedness. Any cash received will be posted to the cash book and to the customer's account to reduce their liability. The balance column on the account provides the current balance owed by the customer.

Chapter five
Double-entry bookkeeping

List of topics

1. Purchases
2. Recording business transactions
3. Goods returns
4. Payment to creditors
5. Payment from debtors

Introduction

This chapter provides an introduction and examination of the system of double entry for recording business transactions, which underpins the system of accounting and financial reporting. Throughout the chapter, students are taken through the double-entry system for reporting cash and credit transactions. The chapter also examines the double-entry system for reporting the return of goods and the payment for credit purchases and sales.

debit
An entry on the left-hand side of an account in the double-entry bookkeeping that denotes an expense in the profit and loss account or an asset in the balance sheet.

credit
An entry on the right-hand side of an account in double-entry bookkeeping that denotes an income in the profit and loss account or a liability in the balance sheet.

1. Purchases

Double entry forms the basis of reporting business transaction in accounting systems. Every business transaction is entered twice in the books of accounts. The rationale for this behaviour can be explained as follows: one account receives the value of the transaction and the other account loses the value of the transaction. For example, Jenny Bloggs decides to withdraw £10,000 to buy a car. Jenny's business bank account decreases by £10,000 and her car account would increase by £10,000. This twin recording of the transaction or bookkeeping process is known as double entry. Traditionally, the books of account were divided into two parts. The left-hand side is the **debit** side and the right-hand side the **credit** side. Every transaction will have a debit and a credit entry.

A debit entry is always an increase in asset or an expense. A credit entry is always an increase in a liability, capital or income. Table 5.1 shows how debits and credits affect the different types of accounts.

Table 5.1: Debits and credits

Account type	Debit	Credit
Assets	Increases	Decreases
Liabilities	Decreases	Increases
Owner's capital	Decreases	Increases
Revenues	Decreases	Increases
Expenses	Increases	Decreases

The recording of the double entry for Jenny's car purchase on 1 February 20X4 is shown below.

Car					
Date	**Description**	**Dr**	**Cr**	**Balance**	
1 Feb 20X4	Car	10,000		10,000	Dr
1 Feb 20X4	Balance			3,000	Dr

Bank					
Date	**Description**	**Dr**	**Cr**	**Balance**	
1 Feb 20X4	Car		10,000	10,000	Cr
1 Feb 20X4	Balance			10,000	Cr

The car is an asset account and increases by £10,000. The bank is also an asset account, but decreases by £10,000 as it was used to finance the car purchase. Equilibrium is maintained in the accounting equation as one asset increases by £10,000 while the other asset decreases by £10,000.

Before getting into the rules and operation of double entry, students should remember that the entries will be recorded in the books of account as and when the transactions occur, not when money for these transactions is received or paid out. For example, if a sale is made on credit terms, it will be recorded in the bookkeeping system as a sale even though it may be several weeks before the customer pays for those goods or services.

On the other hand, if goods are purchased on credit, the purchase will be recorded when it is made and not when the goods are actually paid for, i.e. when a valid invoice for the goods or services is received. This means that double-entry bookkeeping follows the accruals concept discussed in Chapter 2.

Students will have noted that the five account types identified in Table 5.1 are the same as those which comprise the accounting equation:

Capital – (Revenues + Expenses) = Total assets + Total liabilities

You will recall that in order to keep the accounting equation in balance, at least two items in the equation had to be adjusted. Similarly, for each transaction a bookkeeping entry will have to show the impact of a transaction on each of the two items. This means that the bookkeeping system will have one entry showing an increase or decrease in one item, and another entry showing the increase or decrease in the other item. Hence the term 'double-entry bookkeeping' reflects the fact that each entry is made twice.

Worked example 5.1

Monica Lott commenced her small business on 1 June 20X4 and the following transactions took place during the month:

June   Received loan from her father
June   Paid landlord for one month's shop rent
June   Purchased stock of t-shirts
13 June   Received telephone enquiry from client about a future sale
19 June   Purchased shop fittings for cash
27 June   Sold t-shirts for cash

Show the double entry for each transaction.

Answer

Transaction	**Effect**	
	Debit	**Credit**
Received loan from her father	Bank Increases asset	Loan Increases liability
Paid landlord for month's shop rent	Rent Increases asset	Bank Decreases asset
Purchased stock of t-shirts	Stock Increases asset	Bank Decreases asset
Received telephone enquiry from client about a future sale	No effect No transaction	No effect No transaction
Purchased shop fittings for cash	Shop fittings Increases in asset	Cash Decreases asset
Sold t-shirts for cash	Bank Increases asset	Sales Increases revenue

2. Recording business transactions

The remainder of this section explains how the double-entry system is used to record business transactions.

2.1 Purchases

The vast majority of transaction entries in expense accounts reflect an increase in expenses and are recorded on the debit side. A business enters an expense as a debit to increase the business record of what it has spent. For example, on 11 January 20X4 a business purchases cleaning materials at a cost of £200, paying by cheque. The business is decreasing its cash in the bank by £200 and is increasing its expenses by the same amount. These are the two bookkeeping entries – bank is an asset which is being decreased and gets a credit entry, and cleaning materials is an expense which is increased and gets a debit entry.

Cleaning materials				
Date	**Narrative**	**Dr**	**Cr**	**Balance**
11 Jan 20X4	Bank	200		200 Dr
11 Jan 20X4	Balance			200 Dr

Bank				
Date	**Narrative**	**Dr**	**Cr**	**Balance**
11 Jan 20X4	Cleaning materials		200	200 Cr
11 Jan 20X4	Balance			200 Cr

Instead of paying for the cleaning materials by cheque, suppose the business buys them on credit terms from Kleanco. The expense entry stays the same – the expense cleaning materials is increased, or debited. This time, however, the business is not using its bank; but instead the business has increased its liabilities or creditors. To increase a liability account, the business credits it. In short, the balancing entry is credit Kleanco.

Cleaning materials				
Date	**Narrative**	**Dr**	**Cr**	**Balance**
11 Jan 20X4	Kleanco	200		200 Dr
11 Jan 20X4	Balance			200 Dr

Kleanco				
Date	**Narrative**	**Dr**	**Cr**	**Balance**
11 Jan 20X4	Cleaning materials		200	200 Cr
11 Jan 20X4	Balance			200 Cr

2.2 Purchase of fixed assets

When a business purchases a fixed asset, such as a piece of equipment, the fixed asset account, equipment, is debited as it is increased. For example, on 11 January 20X4, a business purchases a computer at a cost of £10,000, paying by cheque. The business is decreasing its cash at the bank by £10,000 and is increasing its fixed assets by the same amount. These are the two bookkeeping entries – bank is an asset which is being decreased and gets a credit entry, and fixed asset (computer) is an asset which is increased and gets a debit.

Fixed asset (computers)				
Date	**Narrative**	**Dr**	**Cr**	**Balance**
11 Jan 20X4	Bank	10,000		10,000 Dr
11 Jan 20X4	Balance			10,000 Dr

Bank				
Date	**Narrative**	**Dr**	**Cr**	**Balance**
11 Jan 20X4	Fixed assets (computers)		10,000	10,000 Cr
11 Jan 20X4	Balance			10,000 Cr

Instead of paying for the computer by cheque, suppose the business agrees to pay 30 days after the computer is installed. The asset entry stays the same – the fixed asset (computer) is increased, or debited. This time, however, the business has increased its liabilities or creditors. To increase a liability account, the business credits it. In short the balancing entry is: debit fixed asset (computers), credit the supplier of the computers Compuco.

Fixed asset (computers)				
Date	**Narrative**	**Dr**	**Cr**	**Balance**
11 Jan 20X4	Compuco	10,000		10,000 Dr
11 Jan 20X4	Balance			10,000 Dr

Compuco				
Date	**Narrative**	**Dr**	**Cr**	**Balance**
11 Jan 20X4	Fixed assets (computers)		10,000	10,000 Cr
11 Jan 20X4	Balance			10,000 Cr

2.3 The asset stock

Stock items are goods purchased for resale. The goods are usually sold at a selling price that is greater than cost price with the difference being profit. If this were not the case, it would be possible for a business to have a stock account with debit entries recording increases (or purchases) in stock and credit entries recording decreases (or sales) in stock. The difference between the debit entries and the credit entries represents the cost of the unsold stock. However, because of the profit element in the sale of stock, this situation does not apply.

Therefore, it is usual to record increases in stock in a purchases account. The purchases account should record only the purchase of goods that the business buys with the prime intention of selling. The purchases account will never record the purchase of items that are bought to be used in the business rather than for resale.

For example, on 11 January 20X4, a business purchases a stock of pens for resale at a cost of £7,500, paying by cheque (see Purchases and Bank ledgers below). Purchases are an expense and an increase in expenses is recorded as a debit entry in the purchases account. Another way of viewing this is to consider the simplest purchase, where the business purchases goods for cash. Making cash purchases decreases cash balance at the bank – credit cash. The balancing entry has got to be a debit entry – debit purchases.

Purchases				
Date	**Narrative**	**Dr**	**Cr**	**Balance**
11 Jan 20X4	Bank	7,500		7,500 Dr
11 Jan 20X4	Balance			7,500 Dr

Bank				
Date	**Narrative**	**Dr**	**Cr**	**Balance**
11 Jan 20X4	Purchases		7,500	7,500 Cr
11 Jan 20X4	Balance			7,500 Cr

Instead of paying for the stock by cheque, suppose the business agrees to pay Penco 30 days after the purchase of the pens. The asset entry stays the same – purchases is increased, or debited. This time, however, the business has increased its liabilities or creditors. To increase a liability account, the business credits it. In short the balancing entry is: debit purchase and credit the supplier of the pens, Penco.

Purchases				
Date	**Narrative**	**Dr**	**Cr**	**Balance**
11 Jan 20X4	Penco	7,500		7,500 Dr
11 Jan 20X4	Balance			7,500 Dr

Penco				
Date	**Narrative**	**Dr**	**Cr**	**Balance**
11 Jan 20X4	Purchases		7,500	7,500 Cr
11 Jan 20X4	Balance			7,500 Cr

Similarly, decreases in stock are recorded in a separate sales account. The sales account should record only the sale of those goods that were bought with the prime intention of resale. It will never record the disposal of other items.

2.4 Sales

Sales are a source of revenue and an increase in revenue is recorded as a credit entry. This can be a difficult concept to understand. A useful way of learning this is to think of the idea that 'making a sale is a credit to the business'. Another way to view the transaction is by thinking of the simplest sale, where the business sells goods for cash.

For example, on 23 January 20X4 a business made a cash sale of £9,000 for its stock that it had purchased for £3,000. A cash sale is an increase in revenue and is recorded as a credit entry in the sales account. Making a cash sale increases cash balance at the bank: debit bank. The balancing entry has got to be a credit entry: crediting sales.

Bank				
Date	**Narrative**	**Dr**	**Cr**	**Balance**
23 Jan 20X4	Sales	9,000		9,000 Dr
23 Jan 20X4	Balance			9,000 Dr

Sales				
Date	**Narrative**	**Dr**	**Cr**	**Balance**
23 Jan 20X4	Bank		9,000	9,000 Cr
23 Jan 20X4	Balance			9,000 Cr

Instead of selling the stock for cash, suppose the business agrees to receive payment 30 days after the sale is made to Buyco. The sales entry stays the same – sales are increased, or credited. This time, however, the business has increased its assets or debtors. To increase an asset account, the business debits it. In short the balancing entry is: debit Buyco (the buyers of the stock), credit sales.

Buyco				
Date	**Narrative**	**Dr**	**Cr**	**Balance**
23 Jan 20X4	Sales	9,000		9,000 Dr
23 Jan 20X4	Balance			9,000 Dr

Sales				
Date	**Narrative**	**Dr**	**Cr**	**Balance**
23 Jan 20X4	Buyco		9,000	9,000 Cr
23 Jan 20X4	Balance			9,000 Cr

3. Goods returns

In business, there are times when buyers have to return the goods they have purchased to the seller; this is a purchase return or return outwards. Conversely, when a seller has goods previously sold to a customer returned to it, this is a sales return, also known as a return inwards.

Intuitively it would appear reasonable to record the purchase return and a sale return as a deduction in the purchase daybook and sales daybook. However, this is wrong and students should never record a purchase or sales return in the purchase daybook or the sales daybook. Two separate accounts must be opened: a purchase return and a sales return.

3.1 Purchase return

A **purchase return** or return outward arises when a purchaser returns to a supplier goods previously bought from the supplier. The item may be returned for a range of different reasons including damage in transit, faulty, wrong item, unfit for purpose or wrong colour. When a business has to return an item of stock to its supplier, this reduces its asset. The return of stock decreases the liability of the supplier to the purchasing business. The double entry for the increase in liability is shown by a debit to the supplier's account. A reduction in the asset has taken place because of the goods being returned. However, this does not require a credit from the purchases account. The reduction in asset is reflected by a credit to the purchase returns account.

purchase return
Goods returned by a business to its supplier.

For example, on 28 January 20X4, a business returns £10,000 of stock items to its supplier Cellco. There are the two bookkeeping entries. The reduction of the stock item is a reduction in an asset. This is shown by a credit in the purchase returns account. The reduction in the liability to the supplier is a debit to the supplier account.

Cellco				
Date	**Narrative**	**Dr**	**Cr**	**Balance**
28 Jan 20X4	Purchase returns	10,000		10,000 Dr
28 Jan 20X4	Balance			10,000 Dr

Purchase returns				
Date	**Narrative**	**Dr**	**Cr**	**Balance**
28 Jan 20X4	Cellco		10,000	10,000 Cr
28 Jan 20X4	Balance			10,000 Cr

3.2 Sales return

sales return
Goods returned to a business by its customers.

A **sales return** or return inwards arises when goods previously sold by a business are returned by a customer. The return of the item reduces the income of the business in receipt of the returned goods. Alternatively, the business experiences an increase in an asset as its stock has increased. The business returning the goods experiences a decrease in assets and a decrease in liability to the business selling the goods.

The double entry required for the sales return is a debit to the sales return account and a credit from the customer's account.

For example, on 30 January 20X4, a business had £2,450 of stock items returned to them by a customer, Spendko. There are the two bookkeeping entries. The increase in the stock is an increase in an asset. This is shown by a debit in the sales return account and a credit to the customer account, Spendko.

Sales return				
Date	**Narrative**	**Dr**	**Cr**	**Balance**
30 Jan 20X4	Spendko	2,450		2,450 Dr
30 Jan 20X4	Balance			2,450 Dr

Spendko				
Date	**Narrative**	**Dr**	**Cr**	**Balance**
30 Jan 20X4	Sales return		2,450	2,450 Cr
30 Jan 20X4	Balance			2,450 Cr

Test yourself 5.1

For each of the following transactions, identify which accounts will receive the debit and credit entry.

	Debit	Credit
1. Purchased a computer from Computazz on credit		
2. Stock sold for cash		
3. Purchased goods on credit from Zin		
4. Sold goods on credit to Dimby		
5. Sold some office furniture for cash		
6. Purchased computer software for cash		
7. A Payne, a long-standing customer, returned some goods purchased last month		
8. Purchased computer table for cash		
9. Sold office fittings on credit to Bizco		
10. Returned some of goods bought from Zin		

4. Payment to creditors

A creditor arises when payment for goods or services are deferred until a later date. The seller of the goods is a creditor of the business buying the goods.

When payment is made to a creditor, the payee will experience a reduction in its asset, as payment will involve a reduction in its bank account or cash account. The payment to the creditor will reduce the liability. To reduce a liability requires a debit to the liability account. The double entries to reduce a liability account are debit liability account and credit bank (or cash) account. The same applies if the business only wishes to discharge a proportion of the total liability. If the business wants to discharge its liability to Kleanco on 31 January 20X4 from its bank balance of £5,000, debit Kleanco and credit bank. The credit of the bank account reduces the asset.

Kleanco				
Date	**Narrative**	**Dr**	**Cr**	**Balance**
11 Jan 20X4	Cleaning materials		200	200 Cr
11 Jan 20X4	Balance			200 Cr
30 Jan 20X4	Bank	200		Nil
30 Jan 20X4	Balance			Nil

Bank				
Date	Narrative	Dr	Cr	Balance
11 Jan 20X4	Balance			5,000 Dr
30 Jan 20X4	Kleanco		200	4,800 Dr
30 Jan 20X4	Balance			4,800 Dr

The total assets held by the business remains unchanged at £4,800 after paying its creditor, although the bank balance has decreased.

Prior to discharging its liability, the business had a bank balance of £5,000 and an outstanding liability of £200, which was a net current asset position of £4,800. Following the payment of the outstanding current liability, the business has a cash balance of £4,800. This business is the same net position as it was prior to its payment of its current liability. The only change has been the elements of its net position. Prior to the payment the net current asset position was as follows:

Bank (£5,000) – Current liability (£200) = Net current asset (£4,800).

After the payment of the current liability, the net current asset position is as follows:

Bank (£4,800) – Current liability (£0) = Net current asset (£4,800).

5. Payment from debtors

On 31 Jan 20X4 Buyco made a payment of £8,000. The £8,000 payment from Buyco will increase the assets of its supplier, with an increase in their bank balance. The balance on Buyco's account will decrease, reduction in an asset – debtors. The accounting entries are debit bank and credit Buyco.

Buyco				
Date	Narrative	Dr	Cr	Balance
23 Jan 20X4	Sales	9,000		9,000 Dr
23 Jan 20X4	Balance			9,000 Dr
31 Jan 20X4	Supplier's Bank		8,000	1,000 Dr
31 Jan 20X4	Balance			1,000 Dr

Bank				
Date	Narrative	Dr	Cr	Balance
23 Jan 20X4	Balance			0
30 Jan 20X4	Buyco	8,000		8,000
31 Jan 20X4	Balance			8,000

Test yourself 5.2

a) **When a customer pays for goods they purchased on credit, what are the correct book entries to record their payment?**

	Debit	Credit
A	Customer's account	Sales account
B	Customer's account	Bank account
C	Bank account	Customer's account
D	Sales account	Bank account

b) **When a business buys fixed asset on credit, what are the correct book entries?**

	Debit	Credit
A	Fixed asset account	Bank account
B	Fixed asset account	Supplier account
C	Supplier account	Fixed asset account
D	Bank account	Fixed asset account

Worked example 5.2

Monica Lott started her small business on 1 June 20X4 with a cash investment of £5,400. The transactions in her first month were as follows:

June	Received £10,000 loan from her father
June	Received £3,000 invoice from landlord for one month's shop rent
June	Purchased £12,000 stock of t-shirts on credit from T-shirt.com
10 June	Sold t-shirts on credit to Bluze for £5,570
13 June	Received telephone enquiry from client which would result in sales of £4,528
15 June	Returned £3,000 of damaged t-shirts to T-shirt.com
19 June	Purchased shop fittings for cash £1,798
21 June	Purchased computers on credit from Komputaz for £1,175
27 June	Sold 90 t-shirts at £21 each, settled by cheque
28 June	Bluze returned £1,000 of damaged t-shirts to Monica
28 June	Paid T-shirt.com £4,000
29 June	Bluze paid £3,500

Produce the ledger accounts for Monica's new business for the month of June 20X4 and show the account balances as at 30 June 20X4.

Answer

Bank					
Date	**Description**	**Dr**	**Cr**	**Balance**	
1 Jun 20X4	Capital	5,400		5,400	Dr
2 Jun 20X4	Loan	10,000		15,400	Dr
19 Jun 20X4	Shopfittings		1,798	13,602	Dr
27 Jun 20X4	Sales	1,890		15,492	Dr
28 Jun 20X4	T-shirt.com		4,000	11,492	Dr
29 Jun 20X4	Bluze	3,500		14,992	Dr
30 Jun 20X4	Balance			14,992	Dr

Capital					
Date	**Description**	**Dr**	**Cr**	**Balance**	
1 Jun 20X4	Bank		5,400	5,400	Cr
30 Jun 20X4	Balance			5,400	Cr

Loan					
Date	**Description**	**Dr**	**Cr**	**Balance**	
2 Jun 20X4	Bank		10,000	10,000	Cr
30 Jun 20X4	Balance			10,000	Cr

Rent					
Date	**Description**	**Dr**	**Cr**	**Balance**	
5 Jun 20X4	Landlord	3,000		3,000	Dr
30 Jun 20X4	Balance			3,000	Dr

Landlord					
Date	**Description**	**Dr**	**Cr**	**Balance**	
2 Jun 20X4	Rent		3,000	3,000	Cr
30 Jun 20X4	Balance			3,000	Cr

Purchases (stock)					
Date	**Description**	**Dr**	**Cr**	**Balance**	
8 Jun 20X4	T-shirt.com	12,000		12,000	Dr
30 Jun 20X4	Balance			12,000	Dr

T-shirt.com					
Date	**Description**	**Dr**	**Cr**	**Balance**	
8 Jun 20X4	Purchases (stock)		12,000	12,000	Cr
15 Jun 20X4	Purchase returns	3,000		9,000	Cr
28 Jun 20X4	Bank	4,000		5,000	Cr
30 Jun 20X4	Balance			5,000	Cr

Bluze					
Date	**Description**	**Dr**	**Cr**	**Balance**	
10 Jun 20X4	Sales	5,570		5,570	Dr
28 Jun 20X4	Bluze		1,000	4,570	Dr
29 Jun 20X4	Bank		3,500	1,070	Dr
30 Jun 20X4	Balance			1,070	Dr

Sales					
Date	**Description**	**Dr**	**Cr**	**Balance**	
10 Jun 20X4	Bluze		5,570	5,570	Cr
27 Jun 20X4	Bank		1,890	7,460	Cr
30 Jun 20X4	Balance			7,460	Cr

Purchase returns					
Date	**Description**	**Dr**	**Cr**	**Balance**	
15 Jun 20X4	T-shirt.com		3,000	3,000	Cr
30 Jun 20X4	Balance			3,000	Cr

Shopfittings

Date	Description	Dr	Cr	Balance	
19 Jun 20X4	Bank	1,798		1,798	Dr
30 Jun 20X4	Perrikom		800	998	Dr
30 Jun 20X4	Balance			998	Dr

Fixed assets (computers)

Date	Description	Dr	Cr	Balance	
21 Jun 20X4	Komputaz	1,175		1,175	Dr
30 Jun 20X4	Balance			1,175	Dr

Komputaz

Date	Description	Dr	Cr	Balance	
21 Jun 20X4	Fixed assets (computers)		1,175	1,175	Cr
30 Jun 20X4	Balance			1,175	Cr

Sales returns

Date	Description	Dr	Cr	Balance	
28 Jun 20X4	Bluze	1,000		1,000	Dr
30 Jun 20X4	Balance			1,000	Dr

Chapter summary

- Every business transaction involves two bookkeeping entries: a debit and a credit.
- A debit is an increase in an asset or expense.
- A credit is an increase in liability, income or capital.
- The ledger records all the accounts of the business. There are the personal accounts of the customers and suppliers which are kept in the sales or debtors ledger, and the purchases or creditors ledger, respectively. These ledgers contain an account or record for each customer and supplier.

- Impersonal accounts record sales, purchases, wages, depreciation, stocks, fixed assets, capital and liabilities, etc. These accounts are all kept in the nominal ledger. The accounts in the nominal ledger are used for preparing the profit and loss account and balance sheet.
- Cash sales – Dr (debit) cash account and Cr (credit) sales account.
- Credit sales is a two-stage process. Stage one is the purchasing – Dr customer's account and Cr sales account. Stage two is the payment – Dr cash account and Cr customer's account.

Test yourself answers

Test yourself 5.1

	Debit	**Credit**
1. Purchased a computer from Computazz on credit	Fixed asset	Computazz
2. Stock sold for cash	Bank	Sales
3. Purchased goods on credit from Zin	Purchases	Zin
4. Sold goods on credit to Dimby	Dimby	Sales
5. Sold some office furniture for cash	Bank	Fixed asset
6. Purchased computer software for cash	Computer software	Bank
7. A Payne, a long-standing customer, returned some goods purchased last month	Sales returns	A Payne
8. Purchased computer table for cash	Computer table	Bank
9. Sold office fittings on credit to Bizco	Bizco	Fixed assets
10. Returned some of goods bought from Zin	Zin	Purchase returns

Test yourself 5.2

a) C – Bank account Customer's account

b) B – Fixed asset account Supplier account

Part three

Chapter 6
Trial balance to financial statements

Chapter 7
Accounting for fixed assets

Chapter 8
The internal controls

Accounting controls

Overview

How do you move from the ledger accounts to produce the financial statements at the end of the accounting period? This section provides a progressive journey from the ledger accounts to the start of the preparation of the financial statements.

To undertake the journey, Chapter 6 provides an overview of the accounting adjustments that have to be made to a trial balance before year-end financial statements can be produced.

The second chapter in this section, Chapter 7, examines accounting for the purchase, use and disposal of, fixed assets.

Chapter 8 provides an overview of the various internal controls used in conjunction with the double entry to provide a check on the double-entry bookkeeping system. The merits of this system are examined, and limitations of the internal controls are identified.

Learning outcomes

At the end of this Part, you will:

- know about adjustments made to ledger account balances before preparing financial statements
- understand the principles of accounting for fixed (non-current) assets
- understand internal controls within the double-entry bookkeeping system.

Chapter six
Trial balance to financial statements

List of topics

1. Stock adjustments
2. Adjustments for accruals and prepayments
3. Debtor adjustments
4. Discounts

Introduction

This chapter introduces students to the various adjustments that are made to the ledger account balances prior to progressing to the preparation of the annual financial statements to report the annual performance and position of a business. The chapter provides an explanation of why they are necessary and how they are undertaken. The rationale and purpose of the adjustments are examined with the aid of the double-entry system. The individual examination of each adjustment enables students to understand and be able to make sense of the effect and impact of the adjustments upon financial statement reporting.

1. Stock adjustments

During a financial year, it is unlikely that all items purchased for resale will have been sold. The reality is that a business will be left with some items of **stock** in hand at the end of the financial year. At this point a business has to calculate the gross profit for the financial year. This calculation is based on the principle that:

stock
Stocks are made up of goods purchased for resale. The intention is to resell the stock, so it will normally be kept in the business for a relatively short time.

Gross profit = Sales – Cost of sales

This calculation is carried out in a section, called the trading account, at the beginning of the profit and loss account. This is discussed in Chapter 9.

The calculation of cost of sales involves important adjustments for opening and closing stocks. These allow the calculation of the cost of goods sold during that period. This can be summarised as follows.

	£
Opening stock	X
Plus Purchases	Y
	x+y
Less Closing stock	Z
Cost of sales	x+y–z

The cost of sales can then be compared to the sales for the financial year and the gross profit can be calculated as follows.

Worked example 6.1

Victoria Goode owns a small cleaning business and her financial year ends on 31 December 20X4. An extract from Victoria's ledger account balances is set out below.

	£
Purchases	5,920
Sales	18,460
Stock at 1 January 20X4	3,600

Stock as at 31 December 20X4 was valued at £2,500.

Prepare a statement to show the cost of sales for the year ending 31 December 20X4.

Answer

	£
Opening stock at 1 Jun 20X4	3,600
Purchases	5,920
	9,520
Closing stock at 31 Dec 20X4	2,500
Cost of sales	7,020

1.1 Accounting for stock

The double entry for the purchase of stock is debit purchases and credit bank (if stock is purchased for cash) or credit supplier account (if stock is purchased on credit).

The transfer of stock to the trading account where stock is an expense requires the following double entry:

Dr Trading account
Cr Purchases account

At the end of the year, the unused stock returns to the stock account from the trading account and the resulting double entry is as follows:

Dr Stock account
Cr Trading account

The stock transferred from the trading account at the year-end is effectively the closing stock at the end of the accounting period. This will be the opening stock at the start of the next accounting period. Therefore the debit to the stock at the end of the period should equal the credit from the stock account at the start of the next accounting period. The double entry at the start of the next accounting period is as follows:

Dr Trading account
Cr Stock account (the value of the closing stock from the previous period)

Sometimes stock held can no longer be sold. This may arise for a variety of reasons, including stock obsolescence (becoming out of date), damage, loss or theft. Consequently, these items of stock have to be written off.

The stock balance has to be adjusted for the non-saleable items of stock. This is explained in Worked example 6.2.

Worked example 6.2

Benny Dee is a computer games retailer and on 1 January 20X4 had a stock of games valued at £25,000. During the year he purchased a further £16,000 of stock items and made £60,000 of sales. When Benny undertook his end-of-year stock check on 31 December 20X4, there was stock valued at original cost of £30,000. However, on further examination, he found stock that had originally cost £1,250 had been damaged and was no longer saleable, plus he learned that owing to a new edition of a computer being released, £5,000 of his stock of the old version was saleable only at half price.

Prepare Benny Dee's cost of sales for the year ending 31 December 20X4.

Answer

Opening stock	25,000
Purchases	16,000
	41,000
Closing stock	26,250*
Cost of sales	14,750

* Closing stock

	Historic cost	Write-off	Realisable value
	£	£	£
Total stock at cost	30,000		30,000
Less			
Damaged stock		1,250	(1,250)
Reduced stock valuation		2,500	(2,500)
Closing stock realisable value			26,250

To compute the closing stock requires a breakdown of the existing £30,000 stock held; £1,250 of the stock is damaged and a further £5,000 has had its saleable value reduced. As you can see, the write-off of the redundant stock is achieved by eliminating its value from the closing stock computation. The prevailing principle is that closing stock must be valued at the lower of cost and **net realisable value**.

net realisable value
The sales value of stock that an organisation expects to receive when the stock is sold. This may be lesser or greater than the cost of the stock owing to deterioration, obsolescence or appreciation over time.

2. Adjustments for accruals and prepayments

We have seen that profit is measured not by comparing 'cash received' during the financial period with 'cash spent', but by matching expenditure incurred with income earned in accordance with the matching principle. The accruals concept states that when computing profit, the sales revenue earned should be matched only against the expenditure incurred when earning it. The sales revenue should be included in the profit and loss account of the period to which it relates, irrespective of when it is received or paid. This principle attempts to ensure that the profit and loss account for a period compares like with like.

2.1 Accrual

An accrual is a cost that has been incurred during the accounting period but which remains unpaid at the end of the period. Alternatively, in terms of benefits, it is a benefit received during the period that remains unpaid at the end of the period.

The problem with accruals and all the adjustments in this section is how to account for them. The main point to remember is that accounting is concerned with when events are incurred and not when payment is made.

It is not uncommon in life and business to enjoy the benefit from a good or service and make payment for its enjoyment at a later date. A common example is payment for the use of utilities or telephone services. The suppliers often invoice at the end of the month or quarter.

An accrual is always an amount that is owing or unpaid at the end of the accounting period. An unpaid balance on an expense account at the end of the accounting period will result in a credit balance on that expense account.

Worked example 6.3

Benny Dee commenced trading on 1 January 20X4 and received his quarterly telephone bills by e-mail on 31 March, 30 June, 30 September and 31 December 20X4. Benny paid his telephone bill within three weeks of its arrival. At the end of the year 31 December 20X4, Benny had one quarter's telephone bill outstanding.

Prepare Benny Dee's telephone account for the year ending 31 December 20X4 and show the position at the year-end.

Answer

Telephone account				
Date	**Description**	**Dr**	**Cr**	**Balance**
31 March 20X4	Telekom Ltd		1,255	1,255
9 April 20X4	Bank	1,255		0
30 June 20X4	Telekom Ltd		2,996	2,996
12 July 20X4	Bank	2,996		0
30 September 20X4	Telekom Ltd		2,427	2,427
10 October 20X4	Bank	2,427		0
31 December 20X4	Telekom Ltd		2,658	2,658
31 December 20X4	Balance			2,658

At the year-end, Benny Dee has a £2,658 credit balance on his telephone account. This reflects the unpaid telephone bill for the last quarter.

At the end of the accounting financial year (or accounting period), a business prepares financial statements consisting of a profit and loss account and a balance sheet. As stated in Chapter 3, the profit and loss account reflects the annual performance, and the balance sheet provides the position as at the year-end.

The profit and loss account will include all the income receivable and expenses payable, whereas the balance sheet will include the balances on all the asset, liability and capital accounts at the year-end date.

Accounting for accruals in the financial statement means that the total expense charged for the year is transferred to the profit and loss account, including the unpaid balance. On the balance sheet, the accrued expense is recorded under the current liabilities.

The explanation for this treatment is the total expense occurred during the financial year and as such is wholly chargeable to profit and loss account. The accrued expense is due for payment at the year-end and is expected to be paid within one financial year, hence it is a current liability.

2.2 Prepayments

A prepayment is the opposite of an accrual. It is the payment for a good or service in the current accounting period, but it will be charged against profit in a later period when the good or service is consumed. Alternatively, a prepayment is the payment for benefit in a period in advance of when the benefit will be received.

The advance payment of an expense results in debit balance on that expense account at the end of the year. This is often found with payment for utilities and property-associated costs such as rent or tax.

Worked example 6.4

Benny Dee's retail business has an accounting year-end date of 31 December 20X4. Benny received an invoice dated 15 March 20X4 for his first year's business insurance of £3,000, with a commencement date of 1 April 20X4. Benny paid the insurance in full via bank transfer on 31 March 20X4.

Prepare Benny Dee's insurance account for the year ending 31 December 20X4 and show the position at the year-end.

Insurance Account				
Date	**Description**	**Dr**	**Cr**	**Balance**
15 March 20X4	Insurance Co		3,000	3,000
29 March 20X4	Bank	3,000		0
31 December 20X4	Balance			0

At the year-end Benny Dee's insurance account shows a nil balance. However Benny has actually made a £750 prepayment. This arises because his insurance year spans 1 April to 31 March, while his accounting year follows a calendar year basis. Therefore, only nine months of any insurance year will relate to the actual accounting year for which the insurance is paid.

The excess of £750 (the prepayment) is transferred to the balance sheet under the heading 'current assets', as it is not due and payable until the next accounting period.

Test yourself 6.1

Benny's balance sheet on 1 January 20X4 included £105 of accrued salaries expenses. During the year ending 31 December 20X4, Benny paid £2,230 for salaries. The accrued salaries on 31 December 20X4 were £75.

a) What was the annual salary expense shown in Benny's profit and loss account for the year ending 31 December 20X4?

A £2,200

B £2,230

C £2,260

D £2,410

Benny's balance sheet on 1 January 20X4 showed rent prepaid at £125. On 31 December 20X4, the prepaid rent was £335. During the year, Benny paid £1,500 in rental payments.

b) What was the annual rental amount shown in Benny's profit and loss account for the year ending 1 January 20X4?

A £1,040

B £1,290

C £1,500

D £1,960

Worked example 6.5

A business has a financial year-end of 31 December 20X4 and it purchases a new car on 1 July 20X4. On that date, the business paid 12 months' vehicle taxation of £180. When preparing its profit and loss account for the year ending 31 December 20X4, the business needs to recognise that the cost of vehicle taxation is for the period 1 July to 31 December 20X4, which would be six months or £90. The other £90 is a prepayment for the following year and should be shown in the balance sheet current assets as a prepayment, or payment in advance.

The adjustments required can be summarised as shown in Table 6.1.

Table 6.1: Year-end adjustments

Year-end adjustment	Definition	Impact on profit and loss account	Impact on the balance sheet
Accruals or expenses owing	The cash payment has been made *after* the benefit has been received.	The relevant expense figure is increased by the amount of the accrual.	Show the amount of the accrual as a current liability on the balance sheet.
Prepayments or payments in advance	The cash payment has been made *before* the benefit has been received.	The relevant expense figure is decreased by the amount of the prepayment.	Show the amount of the prepayment as a current asset on the balance sheet.

3. Debtor adjustments

The realisation concept allows a business to take the profit on credit sales before the cash is received from the debtor. Every time a business sells goods on credit, it is taking a risk that payment may never be received from the debtor. In turn this means that the business is taking a risk in bringing the profit on credit sales into the profit and loss account of the period in which the sale is realised. If the debtor does not pay, the profit for that period will have been overestimated. In order to deal with this uncertainty, accountants can make accounting adjustments which are explained below.

3.1 Bad debts

In general terms, debtors can initially be grouped in two categories: good debtors and bad debtors. Good debtors are those who settle their debt in full and normally within an agreed time frame of, say, 30 days. The cash received from the debtors is reflected in the accounting equation by increasing the cash balance and reducing the debtors' balance.

bad debt
A debt that is or is considered to be uncollectible and is, therefore, written off as a charge to the profit and loss account.

There are some debtors, however, who cannot or will not pay their debts. Those who cannot pay are usually those who become insolvent and go out of business. Those debtors who will not pay are often in dispute with the business – for example, about the quality of the goods or services they have received. These types of debts relate to specific debtors who have failed to pay the debt owed by them. The debt is still owed to the business but the business has to recognise the reality of the situation. It would therefore be appropriate to follow the prudence concept and recognise these as **bad debts**. Consider how imprudent it would be if a debt were seen to be not receivable from the debtor and no adjustments were made; the total debtors' figure appearing under current assets in the balance sheet would be overstated. To provide a more realistic figure of both the financial performance and position of the business, the bad debt should be written off.

Worked example 6.6

A business has trade debtors of £280,000 at the end of the financial year to 31 December 20X4. One of the trade debtors, A. Smith, has owed the business £18,000 for six months. The owner discovers that the debt is likely to be irrecoverable, as Smith has not responded to any reminders and has even moved abroad. The owner decides to treat the £18,000 as a bad debt.

This does not mean simply removing the £18,000 from the debtors balance, as this would ignore the impact of the write-off on the profit earned. The adjustments required are as follows:

1. The bad debt of £18,000 is shown as an expense in the profit and loss account for the year ending 31 December 20X4.
2. The £18,000 bad debt is deducted from the total debtors figure in the balance sheet as at 31 December 20X4. The trade debtors figure is now shown as £262,000 (£280,000 less £18,000).

The double entry for the written-off bad debt is:

Dr Bad debt	£18,000
Cr Debtors	£18,000

The double entry for the transfer to the profit and loss account is:

Dr Profit and loss account	£18,000
Cr Bad debt	£18,000

It is common practice for a business to conduct a regular review of debtors' balances throughout the financial year so that when information is received – for example, concerning the bankruptcy of a debtor – the business will accumulate all bad debts to a bad debts expense account during the financial year and then transfer the total to the profit and loss account at the end of the period. The individual debtors' balances are reduced by the individual bad debt written off.

Finally, should the debtor subsequently pay the amount owing, the bad debt expense is reversed in the year the payment is received. This results in the business adding back the amount previously written off as bad debt to the profit in that year.

When the actual payment is received, the double entry required is:

Dr Cash/bank
Cr Profit and loss account

3.2 Provision for doubtful debts

provision for doubtful debts
A provision made for debtors that may be uncollectable at the balance sheet date.

At any time, there is always a risk that debts will not be collected, which makes it difficult to put an exact value on debtors. A prudent business should make a reasonable estimate of how much of the debts may not be collected. This reasonable estimate is called a **provision for doubtful debts** (PDD) and is charged as an expense in the profit and loss account, and the debtors are shown in the balance sheet with the provision deducted.

Worked example 6.7

In Worked example 6.6, bad debts of £18,000 were written off as an expense in the profit and loss account for the year ending 31 December 20X4. This resulted in a balance sheet figure for trade debtors of £262,000. Suppose the business, having looked at the history of the bad debts, estimates 10% of outstanding debtors are likely to be doubtful. The business would then make a provision for doubtful debts in its accounts for the financial year to 31 December 20X4 of £26,200, i.e. 10% of £262,000.

The adjustments required are as follows.

- The increase in provision for doubtful debts of £26,200 is shown as an expense in the profit and loss account for the year ending 31 December 20X4.

The double entry for the transfer to the profit and loss account is:

Dr Profit and loss account	£26,200
Cr Provision for doubtful debts	£26,200

The provision is then deducted from the debtors figure in the balance sheet, i.e. £262,000 – £26,200 = £235,800.

Test yourself 6.2

a) **What is the purpose of a provision for doubtful debts?**

b) **How is a provision for doubtful debts reported in the balance sheet?**

3.3 Changes in the provision for doubtful debts

As the provision for doubtful debts is an estimate, the actual amount of bad debt is likely to be different from the estimate, so it will be necessary to reassess the level of the provision every year.

3.4 Increasing the provision for doubtful debts

A business may increase its provision for doubtful debts if it feels there is a greater risk of debtors not meeting their obligations for a variety of reasons. If this arises, there will be no change in the accounting for the increase in the provision; the double entry remains unchanged:

Dr Profit and loss account
Cr Provision for doubtful debts

However, there is a change in the actual amount charged to the profit and loss account. Only the increase in the provision, the difference between the old provision and new provision, is charged to the profit and loss account.

Worked example 6.8

In Worked example 6.6, bad debts of £18,000 were written off as an expense in the profit and loss account for the year ending 31 December 20X4. This resulted in a balance sheet figure for trade debtors of £262,000. If the business, having looked at the history of the bad debts, increases its estimates to 15% of outstanding debtors as being likely to be doubtful, the business would make a provision for doubtful debts in its accounts for the financial year to 31 December 20X4 of £39,300, i.e. 15% of £262,000. If the balance on the provision for doubtful debts account was £26,200, the adjustments required are as follows.

- An increase in provision for doubtful debts of £13,100 (£39,300 – £26,200) is shown as an expense in the profit and loss account for the year ending 31 December 20X4.
- The trade debtors balance is now £262,000 less £39,300.

3.5 Reducing the provision for doubtful debts

A business may reduce its provision for doubtful debts if it feels more confident of its debtors meeting their obligations. If this arises, the new double entry will be:

Dr Provision for doubtful debts
Cr Profit and loss account

In addition, the amount of the provision for doubtful debts will also change. The amount charged to the profit and loss account will be the reduction in the provision, the difference between the old provision and new provision.

Worked example 6.9

In Worked example 6.6, bad debts of £18,000 were written off as an expense in the profit and loss account for the year ending 31 December 20X4. This resulted in a balance sheet figure for trade debtors of £262,000. If the business, having looked at the history of the bad debts, reduces its estimates to 2.5% of outstanding debtors as being likely to be doubtful, the business would make a provision for doubtful debts in its accounts for the financial year to 31 December 20X4 of £19,650, i.e. 7.5% of £262,000. If the balance on the provision for doubtful debts account was £26,200, the adjustments required are as follows:

- A reduction in the provision for doubtful debts of £6,550 (£26,200 – £19,650) is shown as a credit in the profit and loss account for the year ending 31 December 20X4.
- The trade debtors balance is now £262,000 less £19,650.

When there is a change in the annual provision for doubtful debts, only the difference between the new provision and the old provision is:

- debited or credited to the profit and loss account; and
- credited or debited to the provision for doubtful debts account.

4. Discounts

trade discount
A reduction in selling price given to customer at the point of sales.

settlement discount
A reduction in an invoice granted to a customer in exchange for early payment.

Two types of discounts can be found in a business: **trade discount** and **settlement discount**.

4.1 Trade discount

A trade discount is a discount granted to a buyer usually for the bulk purchase of items. A trade discount is known at the time of the transaction and has no impact on the accounting system. For example, a seller may grant a buyer a 10% trade discount on the understanding that the purchaser will buy a certain volume of items. The 10% discount is determined before the buyer completes the transaction and it is the discounted price that is recorded in the double-entry system as a standard transaction.

4.2 Settlement discount

Sometimes sellers offer buyers a discount if they pay their invoice in a shorter period than the standard credit term. This incentive to pay an invoice early is a settlement discount. A buyer may get a 5% discount if they settle their invoice in 14 days rather than 30 days. A settlement discount impacts on the double-entry system when the buyer takes the discount. The reverse also applies when a business chooses to settle its debts earlier than contractually agreed. This generates two further discount types: discount allowed and discount received.

Discount allowed
A discount allowed is the value of the discount that a seller grants to a buyer for early settlement.

Worked example 6.10

Benny Dee sold £1,000 of goods to A. Kapp on 20 June 20X4. On 25 June, A. Kapp made a bank transfer to Benny Dee's bank account to take advantage of the 10% discount for payment within 14 days.

The double-entry transactions are in two stages:

1. Actual payment received:

Dr	Bank	£900
Cr	A Kapp	£900

2. Discount allowed:

Dr	Discount allowed	£100
Cr	A Kapp	£100

The £1,000 debt of A. Kapp has been settled by cash payment plus the discount received from A. Kapp.

Discount received
A discount received is the cash discount a buyer receives from a supplier when they settle their account early.

Worked example 6.11

Benny Dee purchased £6,000 of goods from Super Cell on 19 April 20X4. On 26 April, Benny Dee settled his account with Super Cell and took advantage of the 7.5% discount for paying the invoice within ten days.

The double-entry transactions are in two stages:

1. Actual payment made:

Dr	Super Cell	£5,550
Cr	Bank	£5,550

2. Discount received:

Dr	Super Cell	£450
Cr	Discount received	£450

The £6,000 liability of A. Kapp has been settled by cash payment plus the discount received from A. Kapp.

Test yourself 6.3

Kimberley Friday has produced the following trial balance from her business for the year ending 31 December 20X4.

	£	£
Bank		1,450
Sales		24,400
Drawings	15,645	
Debtors	6,143	
Capital		5,376
Rent	1,200	
Creditors		2,080
Advertising	2,400	
Purchases	12,918	
Loan		5,000
	38,306	38,306

Notes

1. **On 31 December 20X4, the closing stock balance had a value of £1,292.**
2. **A client owing £1,143 has been made bankrupt.**
3. **An invoice for an advert placed by Kimberley Friday in October 20X4 for the sum of £400 is still outstanding.**
4. **The last payment of rent was for the six months ending 31 March next year.**
5. **The provision for doubtful debts for the year is 6%.**
   a) **Identify and compute the total value of the accruals and prepayments for the year ending 31 December 20X4.**
   b) **Prepare the accounting adjustments for notes 1–5.**
   c) **Prepare Kimberley Friday's ledger balances if Kimberley settled its outstanding debt to their outstanding balance of £2,080 to Fernhead Sports within 12 days and took the early settlement discount of 10%.**

Chapter summary

- Unpaid expenses at the end of the accounting period are known as accruals.
- Expenses overpaid at the end of the accounting period are known as prepayments.
- Accrued expenses are added to the profit and loss account, and recorded under the current liabilities on the balance sheet.
- Prepaid expenses are deducted from the profit and loss account, and recorded under the current assets on the balance sheet.
- Bad debts and provision for doubtful debts are different in nature and require different adjustments in the financial statements.
- Bad debts are a fact in that they comprise debtors who cannot or will not pay their debts.
- A provision for doubtful debts is a reasonable estimate of the value of debts which may not be collected.
- Bad debts relate to specific debtors who the business knows for a fact have failed to pay the debt owed by them.
- A provision for doubtful debts is different from bad debts in that it does not normally relate to specific debtors.
- Trade discounts do not have any impact on the accounting system.
- Settlement discounts affect the accounting system when the discounts are taken by customers or from suppliers.

Test yourself answers

Test yourself 6.1

a) A – £2,200

b) B – £1,290

Test yourself 6.2

a) The provision for doubtful debts is an estimated amount of bad debt that will arise from debtors who were invoiced during the accounting period but may not settle their debts.

b) A provision for doubtful debts is reported in the balance sheet and a deduction is made from the balance sheet for the estimated amount of the debt, which may not be collected. The deduction prevents an over estimation of the debtors balance and expending costs chasing non-collectable debts.

Test yourself 6.3

a) Accruals are expenses that have been incurred in the accounting period that are unpaid at the end of the accounting period.

On 31 December 20X4 the unpaid accounts were:
Advert: £400

Prepayments are expenses, which have been paid for during the accounting period that will be consumed in a subsequent accounting period.

On 31 December 20X4 the prepaid accounts were:
Rent: £240

Rent was paid to 31 March of the following year. Therefore the rent of £1,200 shown in the trial balance covers a period of 15 months. As the year ended at 31 December, there has been an overpayment for three months into the next year. The overpayment is calculated as follows:

$$\frac{£1{,}200}{15} \times 3 = £240$$

b)

1	**Stock**	**£**
	Opening stock	0
	Purchases	12,918
		12,918
	Closing stock	1,292
	Cost of sales	11,626

2	Bad debt	**£**
	Debtors as per trial balance	6,143
	Bad debt	1,143
	Adjusted debtors	5,000

3	Accrual	**£**
	Advertising as per trial balance	2,400
	Unpaid advert	400
	Advertising at 31 Dec	2,800

4	Prepayment	**£**
	Rent as per trial balance	1,200
	Rent 1 Jan–31 Mar	240
	Rent at 31 Dec	960

5	Provision for doubtful debta	**£**
	Debtors as per trial balance	6,143
	Bad debt	1,143
	Adjusted debtors	5,000
	PDD at 6%	300
	Debtors at 31 Dec	4,700

c)

Bank				
Date	**Description**	**Dr**	**Cr**	**Balance**
dd/mm/20X4	Fernhead Sports		1,872	1,872

Fernhead Sports				
Date	**Description**	**Dr**	**Cr**	**Balance**
dd/mm/20X4	Bank	1,872		1,872

Discount received				
Date	**Description**	**Dr**	**Cr**	**Balance**
dd/mm/20X4	Fernhead Sports		208	208

Fernhead Sports				
Date	**Description**	**Dr**	**Cr**	**Balance**
dd/mm/20X4	Discounts allowed	208		208

Chapter seven
Accounting for fixed assets

List of topics

1. Capital and revenue expenditure
2. The nature of depreciation
3. Methods of depreciation
4. Revaluation of fixed assets
5. Disposal of fixed assets
6. Accounting concepts and depreciation

Introduction

This chapter discusses the nature and distinction of capital and revenue expenditure in relation to fixed assets, or non-current assets as they are known under International Accounting Standards (IAS). Fixed assets were introduced in Chapter 3 and this chapter explains how and why the costs of fixed assets are spread over the period that the asset is owned by the business. Spreading the cost is achieved by annual depreciation charges. Two methods of depreciation are described and supported by practical illustrations of their application. These illustrations are used to discuss the impact of depreciation charges on the financial statements. The impact of purchasing and disposing of fixed assets is also illustrated. Throughout the chapter, reference is made to the subjective nature of depreciation and the influence that accounting concepts have on depreciation.

1. Capital and revenue expenditure

Accountants have to distinguish or classify expenditure (and income) into capital and revenue.

1.1 Capital expenditure

Capital expenditure is expenditure that is likely to provide a benefit to the organisation for more than one accounting period/financial year. The key points are as follows.

- The benefits and period of those benefits may be difficult to predict.
- Such expenditure can be defined as increasing the earning capacity of the business.
- Capital expenditure is incurred on the purchase of fixed assets such as land and buildings, plant and machinery, vehicles, and fixtures and fittings. The cost of these fixed assets is, therefore, accounted for over their anticipated useful life.
- Capital expenditure usually involves an annual depreciation charge.
- Capital expenditure is concerned with purchasing high-value, long-term and permanent fixed assets for use in the business. These assets are not bought to be resold.
- Central government capital grants are an example of capital income.
- The principle is that capital grants should be recognised in the profit and loss account so as to match with the expenditure to which they are intended to contribute.

Test yourself 7.1

a) **Which of the following items of expenditure would be classified as an addition to fixed assets?**

A £1,000 spent on building insurance

B £1,250 spent on an annual licence to play music

C £3,000 spent on lighting equipment

D £5,000 spent on stock

b) **If a revenue item of expenditure was incorrectly classified as capital expenditure, what would be the impact of this on the annual profit?**

1.2 Revenue expenditure and income

Revenue expenditure is expenditure that is necessary for the day-to-day operations of the business. The key points are as follows.

- It is expenditure that is likely to provide benefit to the organisation for only the current accounting/financial year and so is charged against profits in the period to which it relates.
- It is a cost used by the organisation in trading.
- Revenue expenditure include running costs such as electricity, business rates, wages and salaries of employees, interest charges, purchase of consumables such as stationery and goods purchased for resale.

Revenue income includes income from the sale of goods to customers, rents received, dividends received, interest received, etc.

1.3 Importance of the distinction

The distinction between capital and revenue items is critical. If capital and revenue items are not classified accurately, the accounting profit will be incorrectly calculated. For example, if a capital expenditure item is included as revenue expenditure, then the annual profit will be understated. Similarly, if a capital grant were included in one year's accounts, then the annual profits would be overstated.

2. The nature of depreciation

Depreciation is 'the measure of the cost or revalued amount of the economic benefits of the tangible fixed asset that have been consumed during the period' (FRS 15). Consumption includes the wearing out, using up or other reduction in the useful economic life of a tangible fixed asset whether arising from use, effluxion (passing) of time or obsolescence through either changes in technology or demand for the goods and services produced by the asset.

In referring to useful economic life, the definition implies that the business will need to replace the fixed assets at some time in the future. The assumption is that the business is a 'going concern' and that the fixed assets will need to be replaced to maintain the operating capability of the business.

Depreciation may occur due to:

- use or physical deterioration;
- obsolescence; and/or
- time.

2.1 Depreciation through use or physical deterioration

The continued use of fixed assets, such as a plant and machinery or motor vehicles, will lead to their need for replacement at some time in the future. The duration of each class of item varies but they will all need to be replaced eventually. Their replacement will occur at the end of the item's economic life. Fixed assets depreciate as a result of the wear and tear from their usage.

2.2 Depreciation through obsolescence

Obsolescence arises when a fixed asset is no longer useful because an enhanced or improved model has become available. Obsolescence does not necessarily render the existing fixed asset unworkable. It is just the case that a new model or edition has additional attributes or features. The rate of obsolescence with computer technology in the 21st century is a prime example of this practice. It may also be the case that the business has outgrown the fixed asset and requires one with greater functionality as the business has grown.

2.3 Depreciation over time

Fixed assets depreciation over time is specific to fixed assets that have a legal life, such as a lease on a property. As time passes the lease becomes less valuable to the business. At the end of the life of the lease, its value to the leaseholder is nil.

2.4 Depreciation and the accruals concept

Fixed assets are normally purchased for payment in cash. However, accountants do not charge the total cost of the acquisition to one accounting period. Rather, they spread the capital cost over several accounting periods. This is done by gradually writing off the asset's cost in the profit and loss account over several accounting periods corresponding to the asset's useful economic life. This is normally the period over which the present owner of the asset derives economic benefits from its use. The annual charge to the profit and loss account is called depreciation. The total amount to be depreciated is:

Cost – Residual value

The residual value, also known as the scrap value, is what the business expects to realise or receive at the end of the asset's useful economic life. This represents the sale proceeds or trade-in value of the asset. This is in accordance with the accruals concept, as it charges the annual depreciation in the profit and loss and matches it with the revenue sales generated during that same accounting period. This avoids the cost of the acquisition being charged to one accounting period and producing a misleading profit figure. It also recognises that capital expenditure is different from revenue expenditure. The capital expenditure on a fixed asset, unlike expenditure on consumables and services, should not be written off in one year.

Complying with the accruals concept by writing off a fixed asset by an annual depreciation charge is affected by many subjective judgements. There are three key subjective judgements.

1. What is the estimated useful economic life of the fixed asset?
2. What will be the annual use of the fixed asset in each accounting period?
3. What is the estimated residual value?

2.5 Important points regarding depreciation

- As depreciation is an annual charge, it links capital expenditure to revenue expenditure in the profit and loss account and balance sheet.
- The aim of depreciation is to recoup the investment in fixed assets and to spread the cost of the fixed asset over the life of the asset.
- Depreciation is in accordance with the accruals concept, matching revenue earned with expenditure (including depreciation) incurred in generating the revenue.
- Capital expenditure, because of the financial size of a transaction, can have a significant impact on cash flow.
- The annual depreciation charge is a bookkeeping entry in both the profit and loss account and the fixed asset account, which does not involve a cash payment.

- The accounts of a business are expected to show a 'true and fair view' of the financial position. Reduced values cannot therefore be ignored.
- The summation of each year's annual depreciation is termed as the accumulated depreciation charge.
- The original cost of an asset less its accumulated depreciation charge is recorded and shown on the balance sheet as the Net Book Value (NBV).
- The NBV represents the carrying value of an asset on the balance sheet and is often referred to as the 'carrying value'.

Test yourself 7.2

Identify three estimates or judgements that have to be made in order to calculate a depreciation charge.

3. Methods of depreciation

The various methods in use give different arithmetical results in each accounting year, but are related to assumptions about the fixed asset concerning: the estimated useful economic life; the estimated residual value; and the estimated annual use of the fixed asset in each accounting period.

straight-line method
A method of depreciation that remains fixed over the life of the fixed asset.

reducing-balance method
A method of depreciation that reduces annually over the life of the fixed asset.

There are several different methods of calculating depreciation. However, IFA Accounting students will only need to have an understanding of the following two methods: the **straight-line method** and the **reducing-balance method**.

The two methods are illustrated using the following example.

A firm acquires a piece of machinery on 1 January 20X4 at a cost of £60,000. Its estimated useful life is four years and it is anticipated that it can be sold for £14,400 at the end of this period. The percentage rate to reduce the value from £60,000 to £14,400 over four years is 30%.

3.1 The straight-line method

As the name suggests, the total depreciable amount is charged in equal instalments in each accounting period over the expected useful life of the asset. This is the most commonly used method.

The formula for the annual depreciation charge is as follows:

$$\frac{\text{Cost of asset} - \text{Residual value}}{\text{Expected useful life of the asset}}$$

The annual depreciation that is charged is often expressed at the rate of X% per annum on the net cost of the asset. For example, spreading the depreciable amount over four years uses a rate of 25% per annum.

Worked example 7.1

Using the information above:

$$\text{Annual charge} = \frac{\text{Asset cost} - \text{Residual value}}{\text{Live in years}}$$

$$= \frac{£60,000 - £14,400}{4}$$

= £11,400 per annum or 25% of the depreciable amount

Across the life of the asset depreciation is calculated as follows using the straight line method:

	£
Cost as at year 1	60,000
Depreciation year 1	11,400
Net book value as at end of year 1	48,600
Depreciation year 2	11,400
Net book value as at end of year 2	37,200
Depreciation year 3	11,400
Net book value as at end of year 3	25,800
Depreciation year 4	11,400
Net book value as at end of year 4	14,400

3.2 The reducing-balance method

This method of depreciation calculates the annual depreciation charge as a fixed percentage of the **net book value** of the asset, as at the end of the previous accounting period. The net book value (NBV) is the historical cost of an asset less any accumulated depreciation from the date the asset was acquired. In order to arrive at the percentage, accountants use a formula, but students are not required to learn this formula.

net book value
The historic cost of an asset less any accumulated depreciation or other provision for the diminution in value, e.g. reduction to net realisable value.

Worked example 7.2

Across the life of the asset, depreciation is calculated as follows using the reducing-balance method:

	£
Cost as at year 1	60,000
Depreciation year 1 (30% × cost)	18,000
Net book value as at end of year 1	42,000
Depreciation year 2 (30% × net book value)	12,600
Net book value as at end of year 2	29,400
Depreciation year 3 (30% × net book value)	8,820
Net book value as at end of year 3	20,580
Depreciation year 4 (30% × net book value)	6,174
Net book value as at end of year 4	14,406

Under the reducing-balance method, the annual charge for depreciation is higher in the earlier years of the asset's life and lower in the later years. The reducing-balance method might therefore be used when it is considered fair to allocate a greater proportion of the total depreciable amount to the earlier years and a lower proportion to later years, on the assumption that the benefits obtained by the business from using the asset decline over time. It can be argued that for some assets – motor vehicles, for example – the actual value of the assets declines quickly in the early years and more slowly in later years. At the same time, the costs of repairs of a motor vehicle tend to increase as the asset gets older. Adopting the reducing-balance method, in which the depreciation charge reduces as the asset gets older, tends to equalise the total cost of the asset over its life.

Test yourself 7.3

a) **On 1 September 20X4, Best Dance School installed new computer equipment for £12,000. The business charges a full year's depreciation in the year in which an asset is purchased. All fixed assets are depreciated at the rate of 25% per annum on the original cost. The accounting year-end is 31 August. What should be the depreciation charge for the computer equipment in Best Dance School's profit and loss account at the end of the second year?**

A £2,250

B £3,000

C £5,250

D £6,750

b) What should be the accumulated depreciation charge for the new computer equipment in Best Dance School's balance sheet at the end of the second year?

A £2,250

B £3,000

C £5,250

D £6,000

3.3 Accounting for depreciation

Depreciation is an annual charge for the consumption of fixed assets. However, the reduction of the asset does not require a credit to the fixed asset account. The charge for depreciation is made to the profit and loss account, and a provision for depreciation account is opened.

The double entry required for the accounting for depreciation is as follows:

Dr Profit and loss account
Cr Provision for depreciation account

The fixed asset account always remains unchanged with the cost of the fixed asset. Depreciation also has an impact on the balance sheet. Tangible fixed assets are always shown at net book value. The net book value of a fixed asset is the historic cost of the fixed asset less the accumulated depreciation of the fixed asset. Accumulated depreciation is the balance on the provision for depreciation account at the end of the accounting period.

Worked example 7.3

Albert Trader purchased a motor vehicle for his business on 1 July 20X4 for £26,000. The accountant always applies a depreciation charge of 25% reducing balance on motor vehicles. Albert's accounting year ends on 31 December 20X4.

The accounting for depreciation for the year is as follows:

Profit and loss account				
Date	**Narrative**	**Dr**	**Cr**	**Balance**
31 Dec 20X4	Provision for depreciation	6,500		6,500

Provision for depreciation				
Date	**Narrative**	**Dr**	**Cr**	**Balance**
31 Dec 20X4	Profit and loss		6,500	6,500

At the end of the year the motor vehicle account is as follows:

Motor vehicle				
Date	**Narrative**	**Dr**	**Cr**	**Balance**
1 Jul 20X4	Bank	6,500		6,500
31 Dec 20X4	Balance			6,500

The fixed asset extract from the balance sheet is as follows:

Fixed asset	**Cost**	**Accumulated depreciation**	**Net book value**
	£	**£**	**£**
Motor vehicle	26,000	6,500	19,500

The motor vehicle cost is the balance from the motor vehicle ledger account. The accumulated depreciation is the balance from the provision for depreciation account. The net book value is the difference between the two balances.

3.4 Impact of depreciation methods on financial statements

The two depreciation methods have different effects on the figures that appear in both the profit and loss account and on the balance sheet. Over the four-year period, the total depreciation charged to the profit and loss account is the same (£45,600) using both methods. Similarly, at the end of year 4 the net book value of the machine is the same (£14,400). However, it is the different ways of apportioning the depreciation over the useful life of the asset that have an impact on the financial statements. In general terms, the impact is revealed in two ways:

1. The annual depreciation expense charged to the profit and loss account differs for both methods. This will have an impact on the annual profit figure.
2. The value of fixed asset in the accounts as revealed in the balance sheet by the net book value differs in both methods. This will impact on the value of the total assets included in the balance sheet.

Tables 7.1 and 7.2 illustrate the impact.

Table 7.1: Straight-line method

Year	Annual depreciation charged to profit and loss account	Cost of fixed asset	Accumulated depreciation	Net book value included in balance sheet
	£	£	£	£
1	11,400	60,000	11,400	48,600
2	11,400	60,000	22,800	37,200
3	11,400	60,000	34,200	25,800
4	11,400	60,000	45,600	14,400

- This method assumes that the business enjoys equal benefits from the use of the asset in every accounting period throughout its useful economic life. Thus it can be argued that it produces a fair allocation of the total depreciable amount across the different accounting periods.
- The straight-line method has the merits of certainty, simplicity and equality of annual charge.
- It is the most widely used method of depreciation.
- It is particularly applicable to such assets as buildings, patents and leases, where time is the important factor in generating the benefits to be gained from the use of an asset.
- The method does not reflect the fact that, normally, the greatest loss in the market value of a fixed asset occurs in the first year of its use.
- The method does not reflect that there can be an unevenness of the loss in the market value of a fixed asset.

Table 7.2: Reducing-balance method

Year	Annual depreciation charged to profit and loss account	Cost of fixed asset	Accumulated depreciation	Net book value included in balance sheet
	£	£	£	£
1	18,000	60,000	18,000	42,000
2	12,600	60,000	30,600	29,400
3	8,820	60,000	39,420	20,580
4	6,180	60,000	45,594	14,406

- The reducing-balance method charges larger depreciation in the earlier years of the asset's life, and smaller amounts in later years.
- The method assumes that the benefits obtained by the business from using a fixed asset reduce over time.
- The method can be used when it is considered appropriate to charge a greater proportion of the total depreciable amount to the earlier years and a lower proportion to later years.
- The reducing-balance method approximates to reality in respect of certain fixed assets, e.g. motor vehicles where the depreciation calculated in the first year reflects the great loss in market value at the same time as when repairs are usually low.

3.5 Choosing a depreciation method

The business should choose the method most appropriate to the business. The method should be one that matches depreciation expense to the revenues that the fixed asset helped to generate. The accountancy bodies in their accounting standard on depreciation do not recommend one method over another. The standard says that the method used should be the one most appropriate to the fixed asset and to the assets used in the business.

Tangible fixed assets
Depreciation is provided, normally on a straight-line basis, to write off the cost or valuation of tangible fixed assets over their estimated useful economic lives to any estimated residual value, using the following rates.

Buildings	up to 50 years
Research equipment	8 years
Computing equipment and motor vehicles	3–5 years
Other equipment	10–15 years

No depreciation is provided on freehold land and assets in the course of construction.

Test yourself 7.4

a) Provide a brief outline of why it is necessary to depreciate tangible fixed assets.

b) Outline the difference between the straight-line method and the reducing-balance method of depreciation.

4. Revaluation of fixed assets

Whatever method is chosen, depreciation is calculated using the historical cost of the fixed asset. The fact is, however, that the value of many fixed assets, particularly some land and buildings, rises over time, largely because of inflation.

Some organisations periodically revalue their fixed assets to reflect the current market value, otherwise the total value of the assets might seem unrealistically low. The depreciation is then calculated on the revalued amount. The impact of the revaluation of fixed assets on the accounting equation is reflected in a corresponding increase in the owner's capital funds.

5. Disposal of fixed assets

In the normal course of trading, a business purchases and resells its fixed assets. This maintains the operating capability of the business as a going concern. The asset to be sold is recorded in the balance sheet at its net book value, i.e. its historic cost less depreciation to the date of sale. It is important to remember that the net book value does not represent an estimate of its market value. Net book value is an asset's value to the business. The proceeds of the sale are thus likely either to exceed or to be less than the net book value. This will result in either a paper profit or loss.

The accounting for the disposal of a fixed asset can be separated into four stages:

1. Open a fixed asset disposal account.
2. Transfer the fixed asset for sale to the disposal account.
3. Transfer the depreciation for the fixed asset being sold to the disposal account.
4. Credit any proceeds of the sale to the disposal account.
5. Transfer any gain or loss arising from the disposal to the profit and loss account.

The ledger entries to account for the disposal of fixed assets are as shown in Table 7.3.

Table 7.3: Ledger entries for the disposal of fixed assets

No.	Ledger entries	Explanation
1	Dr Disposal account Cr Fixed asset account	Write out the original cost of the fixed asset from the fixed asset account to the disposal account.
2	Dr Provision for depreciation Cr Disposal account	Write out the accumulated depreciation for the disposed fixed asset from the provision for depreciation account to the disposal account.
3	Dr Bank Cr Disposal account	Record the proceed of the sale of the fixed asset.
4	Transfer the loss to the profit and loss account from the disposal account	The profit or loss on sale of fixed asset is transferred to the profit and loss account.

Worked example 7.4

Aztex Traders' accounting year-end is 30 June and uses straight-line depreciation for their plant and machinery. The business does not charge for depreciation in the year of disposal. On 15 January 20X4, plant and machinery was purchased for £26,000. The expected life of the plant and machinery was five years and the expected residual value was £1,000.

On 2 July 20X4, Aztex Traders received an offer from Zippo Plant Ltd to purchase Aztex's plant and machinery for £12,000. Aztex Traders want to know if they should accept the offer. The explanation should show the ledger accounts.

The ledger entries for the offer of £12,000 from Zippo Plant are as follows:

Disposal account				
Date	**Narrative**	**Dr**	**Cr**	**Bal**
		£	**£**	**£**
2 July 20X4	Plant and machinery	26,000		26,000
2 July 20X4	Depreciation		5,000	21,000
2 July 20X4	Bank		12,000	9,000
2 July 20X4	Transfer to profit and loss		9,000	0

Plant and machinery				
Date	**Narrative**	**Dr**	**Cr**	**Bal**
		£	**£**	**£**
30 June 20X4	Balance	26,000		26,000
2 July 20X4	Disposal		26,000	0

Provision for depreciation				
Date	**Narrative**	**Dr**	**Cr**	**Bal**
			£	**£**
30 June 20X4	Balance			5,000
2 July 20X4	Disposal	5,000		0

Profit and loss				
Date	**Narrative**	**Dr**	**Cr**	**Bal**
		£	£	£
2 July 20X4	Disposal	9,000		9,000

If Aztex Traders accept the offer from Zippo Plant, they would make a loss of £9,000. This is shown by a debit balance on the disposal account. The balance on the disposal account is transferred to the profit and loss account. As it is a loss on the sale of a fixed asset, the double entry is:

Dr Profit and loss account
Cr Disposal account

Worked example 7.5

Aztex Traders, accounting year-end is 30 June and uses the reducing-balance depreciation method for their computer equipment at a rate of 50% per annum. The business does not charge for depreciation in the year of disposal. On 3 August 20X4, computer equipment was purchased for £64,000.

On 12 September 20X4, Aztex Traders received an offer from Recykle IT to purchase Aztex's computer equipment for £18,000. The owner's immediate response was to reject the offer. Advise Aztex Traders whether the offer should be accepted. Your advice must show the ledger accounts.

The ledger entries for the offer of £18,000 from Recykle IT are as follows:

Disposal account				
Date	**Narrative**	**Dr**	**Cr**	**Bal**
		£	£	£
12 September 20X4	Computer equipment	64,000		64,000
12 September 20X4	Depreciation		48,000	16,000
12 September 20X4	Bank		18,000	2,000
12 September 20X4	Transfer to profit and loss	2,000		0

Computer equipment				
Date	**Narrative**	**Dr**	**Cr**	**Bal**
		£	**£**	**£**
30 June 20X4	Balance	64,000		64,000
12 September 20X4	Disposal		64,000	0

Provision for depreciation				
Date	**Narrative**	**Dr**	**Cr**	**Bal**
		£	**£**	**£**
30 June 20X4	Balance			48,000
12 September 20X4	Disposal	48,000		0

Profit and loss				
Date	**Narrative**	**Dr**	**Cr**	**Bal**
		£	**£**	**£**
12 September 20X4	Disposal		2,000	2,000

If Aztex Traders accept the offer from Recykle IT, they would make a profit of £2,000. This is shown by a credit balance on the disposal account. The balance on the disposal account is transferred to the profit and loss account. As it is a profit on the sale of a fixed asset, the double entry is:

Dr Disposal account
Cr Profit and loss account

Obviously organisations purchase and sell assets at various times throughout the financial year. It is possible to calculate a proportionate amount of depreciation to reflect accurately when an asset was sold or purchased. This reflects the limited amount of use the business has had from the asset in that period. In practice, many organisations ignore the part-year depreciation, and charge a full year's depreciation on fixed assets in the year of their purchase (regardless of the point in time during the year at which they were acquired) and no depreciation in the year of sale/disposal of the asset. While a failure to apportion depreciation to the months of the year when an asset is only owned for a few months is actually contrary to the matching concept, it may be defended on the grounds of materiality (see Chapter 2, Materiality, page 20).

Test yourself 7.5

a) **Mexi Bend's financial year-end is 31 December. On 1 January 20X4, an item of fixed asset was purchased for £12,000 and then depreciated by 20% per annum using the reducing balance method. The fixed asset was sold on 1 January 20X7 for £6,000. There is depreciation charged in the year of disposal. The sale on 1 January 20X7 results in which one of the following?**

A A loss on disposal of £1,200

B A loss on disposal of £144

C A profit on disposal of £144

D A profit on disposal of £1,200

b) **On 1 January 20X4, BEC Ltd had fixed assets with a total cost of £250,000, and the accumulated depreciation was £125,000. A van with an original cost of £40,000 and accumulated depreciation of £18,250 was sold for £15,000. Depreciation is charged at a rate of 20% per annum, on the reducing-balance method. Depreciation is not charged in the year of disposal of an asset.**

Prepare the disposal account, fixed asset account, provision for depreciation account and profit and loss account to reflect the disposal of the van on 1 January 20X4.

5.1 Intangible fixed assets

There are a number of aspects of a business that may not have a monetary value placed on them. These include:

- a skilled, loyal and efficient workforce;
- excellent relations between management and the workforce;
- the site of a business (for example, if this is in a city centre or near a motorway, it may give the business a competitive advantage);
- a range of well-known and trusted brand names;
- a range of products or services protected by patents or copyrights; and
- a loyal customer base built up by the business's relations with customers.

These are all intangible assets and, as we saw in Chapter 3, they are difficult to identify in monetary terms on a balance sheet, but they would nevertheless be valued by a prospective buyer. Intangible assets are frequently created or built up in the course of time by a business. The value of such intangible assets is not usually included in the balance sheet, as accountants cannot place an objective value on them.

6. Accounting concepts and depreciation

Most managers do not need to be caught up in the technical aspects of depreciation but will need to understand the reasons why depreciation is included and its impact on financial statements. This approach is assisted by recognising that the recording of depreciation in financial statements is greatly influenced by the application of accounting concepts as follows:

- The historic cost concept directs that transactions, e.g. the purchase of fixed assets, are recorded at the value at the time the transaction occurred.
- The going concern concept directs that assets are not recorded at their break-up value, as it is assumed the business will continue in existence.
- The matching/accruals concept directs that the main objective of depreciation is to match the cost of the fixed asset against the revenue that the asset is helping to generate.
- The consistency concept directs that the accounting treatment of depreciation should involve a method that is used consistently and gives comparability over accounting periods.

Test yourself 7.6

a) On 1 September 20X2, Betta Printers purchased new equipment at a cost of £14,000. The business charges a full year's depreciation in the year an asset is purchased. All fixed assets are depreciated at the rate of 25% per annum on a reducing balance basis. The accounting year-end is 31 August.

Calculate the annual depreciation charge for the equipment in Betta Printers' profit and loss account at the end of the second year.

b) Calculate the accumulated depreciation charge for the equipment shown in Betta Printers' balance sheet at the end of the second year.

c) Explain the following terms:

i) 'net book value'

ii) 'residual value' in relation to fixed assets.

Chapter summary

- The distinction between capital and revenue income and expenditure is important within the accounting process.
- Capital expenditure is money spent on an item that will create a fixed asset.

- Capital expenditure invariably gives rise to depreciation charges after the purchase process has been completed.
- Revenue income arises from operational trading activities during the course of an accounting period.
- Revenue expenditure is expenditure incurred on operational activities within an organisation or business.
- Depreciation is the accounting for the consumption of fixed assets during an accounting period.
- Fixed assets have a lifespan and benefit to a business over one year.
- Depreciation may arise through use, obsolescence or overtime.
- The straight-line method of depreciation results in a fixed annual depreciation charge to the financial statement throughout the life of the asset.
- The reducing-balance method of depreciation results in a fixed annual percentage depreciation charge to the financial statement throughout the life of the asset.

Test yourself answers

Test yourself 7.1

a) C – £3,000 spent on lighting equipment

b) The accounting profit would be understated.

Test yourself 7.2

Annual usage of the asset, estimated economic life and estimated residual value.

Test yourself 7.3

a) B – £3,000

b) D – £6,000

Test yourself 7.4

a) Tangible fixed assets are depreciated because their costs are not charged to the entity on acquisition because they have a life span beyond one year. Consequently, their accounting cost is spread over their useful life. Methods of depreciation are used to spread the accounting cost of tangible fixed assets over their useful life.

b) The straight-line method of depreciation results in a fixed annual charge being made to the profit and loss account over the life of the asset. The reducing-balance method of depreciation results in a decreasing annual made to the profit and loss account over the life of the asset.

Test yourself 7.5

a) B – A loss on disposal of £144

Fixed asset

	Dec 20X4	Dec 20X5	Dec 20X6
	£	£	£
Cost	12,000	12,000	12,000
Depreciation b/f	0	2,400	4,320
Annual depreciation	2,400	1,920	1,536
Depreciation c/f	2,400	4,320	5,856
NBV	9,600	7,680	6,144
Sales proceeds			
1 Jan 20X7			6,000
Profit on disposal			(144)

b) On 1 January 20X4, BEC Ltd had fixed assets with a total cost of £250,000, and the accumulated depreciation was £125,000. A van with an original cost of £40,000 and accumulated depreciation of £18,250 was sold for £15,000. Depreciation is charged at a rate of 20% per annum, on the reducing-balance method. Depreciation is not charged in the year of disposal of an asset.

Prepare the depreciation and fixed asset disposal accounts for the year ended 31 December 20X4.

Disposal account

Date	Narrative	Dr	Cr	Bal
		£	£	£
1 January 20X4	Van	40,000		40,000
1 January 20X4	Depreciation		18,250	21,750
1 January 20X4	Bank		15,000	6,750
1 January 20X4	Transfer to profit and loss		6,750	0

Van

Date	Narrative	Dr	Cr	Bal
		£	£	£
1 January 20X4	Balance	40,000		40,000
1 January 20X4	Disposal		40,000	0

Provision for depreciation				
Date	**Narrative**	**Dr**	**Cr**	**Bal**
		£	**£**	**£**
1 January 20X4	Balance			125,000
1 January 20X4	Disposal	18,250		106,750

Profit and loss				
Date	**Narrative**	**Dr**	**Cr**	**Bal**
		£	**£**	**£**
1 January 20X4	Disposal	6,750		6,750

Test yourself 7.6

a) The annual depreciation charge reported in the profit and loss account of Betta Printers on 31 August 20X4 would be £2,625.

b) The accumulated depreciation charge reported in the balance sheet, as at 31 August 20X4 would be £6,125.

	Aug 20X3	**Aug 20X4**
	£	**£**
Cost	14,000	14,000
Depreciation b/f	0	3,500
Annual depreciation	3,500	2,625
Accumulated depreciation	3,500	6,125
NBV	10,500	7,875

c) i) Net book value is the accounting valuation of a tangible fixed asset at the end of an accounting period. This is calculated by the cost of the tangible fixed asset less the accumulated depreciation to date.

ii) Residual value is the estimated valuation of a tangible fixed asset at the end of its economic useful life with an entity.

Chapter eight
The internal controls

List of topics

1. Trial balance
2. Trial balance and errors
3. Bank reconciliation
4. Control accounts

Introduction

This chapter identifies and examines the three elements of internal controls within the double-entry bookkeeping system. The role of the trial balance and the associated errors are examined to demonstrate the importance of the trial balance. The bank reconciliation is examined and its importance in bridging the differences between the cash book and bank account balances is demonstrated using two alternative methods. Finally, the preparation and purpose of the control accounts is discussed. This chapter provides students with an understanding of the three internal controls that exist to ensure the correctness of the double-entry system prior to embarking on the preparation of the final accounts.

1. Trial balance

trial balance
A list of account balances in a double-entry accounting system.

A **trial balance** is a list of the ledger account balances at one point in time. The trial balance lists the ledger accounts and their respective debit or credit balance. As it was established in Chapter 5 that every transaction generates a debit and a credit transaction, a trial balance by definition will result in the total debits and credits being equal. Although a trial balance consists of a list of debit and credit ledger balances based upon the principle of double entry, the trial balance is not a part of the double-entry system. It is just an arithmetical check of the ledger balances, drawn up in two columns: debits and credits. This is important to note, because a trial balance may not be correct even if the total debits equal the total credits. However, this will be examined later in this chapter. An example of a trial balance is shown in Figure 8.1.

T. Smith		
Trial balance as at 31 December 20X4		
	£	**£**
Sales		70,000
Purchases	26,000	
Rent	8,000	
Sundry expenses	7,000	
Loan interest	2,000	
Debtors	2,000	
Cash	22,000	
Buildings	10,000	
Fixtures and fittings	36,000	
Loan		20,000
Creditors		3,000
Capital		20,000
	113,000	113,000

Figure 8.1: Trial balance of a business as at 31 December 20X4

A trial balance is always produced at a point in time and not for a period. Hence it is always titled 'as at', followed by the date for the end of the reporting period. It is customary to produce a trial balance at the end of the accounting period, forming a link between the ledger recording and the accounts production. Alternatively, this may be regarded as the bridge between the end of the bookkeeping process (recording business transactions) and the beginning of the accounting process (reporting of financial information to users in order that they can make economic decisions). Despite the usual practice of producing a trial balance at the end of the accounting period, a trial balance can be produced more frequently to provide an internal check that a business has recorded its business transactions correctly and all its debits are equal to its credits.

Test yourself 8.1

a) **What is a trial balance?**

b) **The sum of the debits of a trial balance always equals the sum of the credits. True or false?**

c) **A trial balance is part of the double-entry bookkeeping system. True or false?**

d) **A trial balance can be drawn up on a weekly basis. True or false?**

Worked example 8.1

The following balances were extracted from the ledgers of ABJ Stores Ltd at the end of the year 30 June 20X4:

ABJ Stores Limited at the end of the year 30 June 20X4

	£
Telephone	1,301
Purchases	21,548
Sales return	1,800
Interest received	1,125
Closing stock	2,156
Equipment	7,500
Bank	2,250
Turnover	36,000
Rent	4,131

Task: You are required to produce a trial balance for ABJ Stores as at 30 June 20X4 and identify the capital balance. (Note: a bank balance is presumed to be an asset (debit balance) unless you are told otherwise.)

Answer

ABJ Stores

Trial balance as at 30 June 20X4

Narrative	**Dr**	**Cr**
	£	**£**
Telephone	1,301	
Purchases	21,548	
Sales return	1,800	
Interest received		1,125
Closing stock	2,156	
Equipment	7,500	
Bank	2,250	
Turnover		36,000
Rent	4,131	
	40,686	37,125
Capital balance		3,561
Total	40,686	40,686

To prepare a trial balance from the information in the question, a student must be able to determine whether the ledger balances are debit or credit balances. A review of the ledger balances would lead to the conclusion that only two of the balances were credit balances: interest received and turnover. There is no doubt or confusion over the bank balance being a debit balance, because if it was a credit balance, the labelling would read 'bank overdrawn'.

The allocation of the ledger balances into their appropriate columns, debits or credits, results in the total debits exceeding the total credits. The difference between the two totals must therefore be the missing capital balance.

Despite the trial balance being an arithmetic check on the ledger balances, it should be noted that a trial balance may still contain errors despite the total debits being equal to total credits.

2. Trial balance and errors

Two types of errors may arise when preparing a trial balance. The first type of error occurs when the total debits and total credits are not equal. This may arise if a transposition error has occurred when recording one or more of the entries. For example, a credit sale to a customer may have taken place for £123, but it may have been entered in one of the ledgers as £132. This error may go unnoticed until the trial balance is drawn up and the debits are found not to equal the credits.

The second type of errors that are found in the trial balance are the ones where the total debits and total credits are still equal. These errors are more concerning as they are not detected by the trial balance. There are six such errors which the trial balance is unable to detect. These errors are:

1. commission
2. omission
3. principle
4. reversal
5. original entry
6. compensation.

2.1 Error of commission

An error of commission occurs when the correct amount has been posted in the ledger but it has been posted to the wrong account. For example, on 1 July 20X4, the bookkeeper at Bizi Business incorrectly debited Alpha Ltd with a £3,000 credit sale, instead of Alfar Ltd.

To correct the error, the following adjustments are required:

Dr Alfar Ltd £3,000
Cr Alpha Ltd £3,000

This correction could be made by the issue of a credit note to Alpha Ltd and an invoice to Alfar Ltd, or through a journal entry.

The debit entry is the correct debtor account from the credit sale and the credit entry cancels out the original incorrect entry into Alpha Inc's ledger account. At the end of the period the double entry should show:

Dr Alfar Inc	£3,000
Cr Sales	£3,000

2.2 Error of omission

An error of omission occurs when a transaction has taken place but it has not been entered in the books of prime entry. The trial balance will balance despite the omitted transaction. For example, on 2 July 20X4, the bookkeeper at Bizi Business did not record the cash purchase of stock for £7,650.

To correct the error, the following adjustments are required:

Dr Stock	£7,650
Cr Cash	£7,650

2.3 Error of principle

An error of principle occurs when a transaction has been posted to the wrong type of account. For example, on 3 July 20X4, £4,125 was paid to FG Insurance Co, but the bookkeeper entered the payment as a debit in the administration account.

To correct the error, the following adjustments are required:

Dr FG Insurance	£4,125
Cr Administration	£4,125

The debit entry is the correct ledger account to be charged with the cost of insurance. The credit entry cancels out the original incorrect entry into the administration account. At the end of the period, the double entry should show:

Dr FG Insurance	£4,125
Cr Bank	£4,125

2.4 Error of reversal of entry

An error of reversal of entry occurs when a transaction is entered in the correct accounts but each item has been entered on the wrong side of each account. For example, on 4 July 20X4, a business purchased £10,000 of fixed assets, but the bookkeeper recorded the correct amount but on the wrong side of the ledger accounts. The bookkeeper's entries are as follows:

Dr Bank	£10,000
Cr Fixed asset	£10,000

To correct the bookkeeper's error, an adjustment in two stages is required. First, the original error has to be cancelled. This requires a reversal of the original entries:

Dr Fixed asset	£10,000
Cr Bank	£10,000

The debit and credit entry cancels the original entries. Both accounts now have a nil balance. This enables the second stage of the adjustment to be undertaken. The second stage of the process is recording the entries on the correct sides of the accounts:

Dr Fixed asset	£10,000
Cr Bank	£10,000

This is the identical recording of the first stage of the process and results in the correct ledger balances at the end of the period.

In effect, this indicates that to adjust an error of reversal of entries requires entries of double the initial incorrect entries. The explanation for a doubling of the original incorrect entry is as follows: the first half of the adjustment eliminates the error and the second half of the adjustment effects the correct transaction.

2.5 Error of original entry

An error of original entry occurs when a transaction is incorrectly recorded in the books of account. For example, on 5 July 20X4, goods purchased for £590 were entered as £950 on both sides of the account. As a result of this error, both ledger accounts are overstated by £360.

The corresponding double-entry transactions required to correct these entries are as follows:

Dr Bank	£360
Cr Goods	£360

Each account is reduced by £360 to bring its balance back to the correct £590.

Students should be aware that the double-entry adjustment required to return each ledger balance to its correct balance would be reversed if the original entry had given rise to an understatement of £360.

2.6 Error of compensation

An error of compensation occurs when an error on one side of the ledger is wholly compensated by an error of equal value on the other side of the ledger. For example, on 6 July 20X4, the bookkeeper incorrectly overstated and entered a sales invoice and purchase invoice by £450.

To correct the bookkeeper's error, the following adjustment is required:

Dr Sales	£450
Cr Purchases	£450

The adjustments reduce the respective ledger balances by the original overstatement.

Test yourself 8.2

a) The bookkeeper at Sun Bakers posted a £500 sales invoice to F. Smith in error. The invoice total was correct but it was for another debtor, T. Smith. This mistake is an error of which kind?

A Principle

B Transposition

C Commission

D Original entry

b) A closer examination of the records of Sun Bakers revealed that a £750 sales invoice to Barbi Khan was entered in the books as £570. This mistake is an error of which kind?

A Principle

B Transposition

C Commission

D Original entry

c) Explain the error of reversal of entry.

d) Explain the difference between a compensation error and an error of principle.

3. Bank reconciliation

At periodic intervals, usually monthly, a business will receive a bank statement. The bank statement shows all the transactions processed through the banking system at the end of the reporting period. The bank statement should mirror the cash book maintained by the business. However, it is uncommon to find agreement between the bank statement and the cash book maintained by a business. The differences between the bank statement and the cash book can occur for a variety of valid or justifiable reasons. The disagreements may arise from timing differences or actual mistakes. These will be examined later in this chapter.

bank reconciliation
A process of comparing the bank statement balance with the cash book balance.

Whatever the source or reason for the differences, a **bank reconciliation** should be prepared at the end of each month. A bank reconciliation is prepared in order to provide an explanation for the difference between the bank statement and the cash book.

Worked example 8.2

A business maintains a cash book and has just received its bank statement for the period ending 30 June 20X4.

Cash book					
Date	**Description**	**Dr**	**Cr**	**Balance**	
1 Jun 20X4	Bal	875		875	Dr
3 Jun 20X4	A Club	453		1,328	Dr
7 Jun 20X4	B Diamonds		345	983	Dr
15 Jun 20X4	C Hearts	654		1,637	Dr
25 Jun 20X4	J Spade		897	740	Dr
28 Jun 20X4	Y Silver		321	419	Dr
30 Jun 20X4	L Gold	699		1,118	Dr
30 Jun 20X4	Balance			1,118	Dr

Bank					
Date	**Description**	**Dr**	**Cr**	**Balance**	
1 Jun 20X4	Bal		875	875	Cr
3 Jun 20X4	Deposit		453	1,328	Cr
7 Jun 20X4	B Diamonds	345		983	Cr
15 Jun 20X4	Chq 2107		654	1,637	Cr
25 Jun 20X4	J Spade	897		740	Cr
30 Jun 20X4	Bank charges	96		644	Cr
30 Jun 20X4	Balance			644	Cr

Prepare a bank reconciliation statement as at 30 June 20X4.

Answer

A review of the cash book and the bank statement highlights two entries in the cash book that are not shown on the bank statement: the last two transactions during the month, the cheque to Y Silver £321, and the deposit lodged on 30 June 20X4. In addition, the bank charges on the bank statement are not shown in the cash book.

To perform a bank reconciliation, the first action required is to update the cash book with the bank charges, £96. Thus the cash book opening balance for the bank reconciliation process is £1,022 as shown below.

Cash book					
Date	**Description**	**Dr**	**Cr**	**Balance**	
1 Jun 20X4	Bal	875		875	Dr
3 Jun 20X4	A Club	453		1,328	Dr
7 Jun 20X4	B Diamonds		345	983	Dr
15 Jun 20X4	C Hearts	654		1,637	Dr
25 Jun 20X4	J Spade		897	740	Dr
28 Jun 20X4	Y Silver		321	419	Dr
30 Jun 20X4	L Gold	699		1,118	Dr
30 Jun 20X4	Bank charges		96	1,022	Dr
30 Jun 20X4	Balance			1,022	Dr

Bank reconciliation statement

As at 30 June 20X4

	£	£
Balance per cash book		1,118
Plus		
Unpresented cheque	321	321
Less		
Bank lodgement not on bank statement	699	
Bank charges	96	795
Balance as per bank statement 30 June 20X4		644

Students should note that the bank account balance is shown as a debit balance in the cash book because the bank balance is an asset. However, the bank account balance is shown as a credit balance. This is not an error. The bank account balance is a liability of the bank to the business. The business would be a creditor in the books of the bank. This is a common misunderstanding for students of accounting.

A bank reconciliation statement may be prepared using two different methods. The first method is as per Worked example 8.2, where the reconciliation begins with the cash book balance and ends with the bank statement. The second method begins with the bank statement balance and ends with the cash book balance. The alternative methods are shown in Figure 8.2.

Method 1

Bank reconciliation statement
As at day month year

	£
Balance as per cash book balance	X
Plus	
Unpresented cheques	
Bank deposit (or credit transfer)	Y
Less	
Bank deposits not yet shown on bank statement	
Bank charges	Z
Balance as per bank statement	X + Y – Z

Method 2

Bank reconciliation statement
As at day month year

	£
Balance as per bank statement	X
Plus	
Bank deposits not yet shown on bank statement	
Bank charges	Y
Less	
Unpresented cheques	
Bank deposit (or credit transfer)	Z
Balance as per cash book	X + Y – Z

Figure 8.2: Alternative bank reconciliation methods

Whichever method is used to prepare a bank reconciliation, the terms and content are the same and require further explanation as they contribute to explain the differences between the cash book and bank statement.

- **Unpresented cheques** are cheques that have been issued to a payee but have not yet been presented to the bank or processed by the banking system.
- A **bank transfer** (credit transfer) is a direct payment into a bank account such as a direct debit or standing order by a customer; the transfer does not appear in the cash book.
- **Bank lodgement not yet bank** is a payment received and entered in the cash book, but it may not have been deposited into the bank or it has not been processed through the bank system at the bank statement date.

3.1 Why do we need bank reconciliations?

It is not customary to find agreement between the cash book and bank statement in the accounting process. Consequently a bank reconciliation is required, as explained in the previous section.

The disagreements may arise for a variety of reasons, which can be separated into three groups: entries on the bank statement only, entries on the cash book only, or errors in the cash book and/or the bank statement.

Entries on the bank statement only

The transactions that may only be entered on the bank statement include:

- bank charges entered on the bank statement;
- bank interest received on the bank statement;
- direct debit or standing order entry on the bank statement;
- income credited directly to the bank account, such as dividends, interest, direct payment from customers; and
- dishonoured cheques shown on the bank statement.

Entries on the cash book only

The transactions that may only be entered on the cash book include:

- income received and entered on the cash book but not yet lodged into the bank account; and
- cheques issued to third parties but not yet processed through the banking system and as such they do not appear on the bank statement.

Errors in the cash book and/or the bank statement

A cash book and a bank statement may contain a numerical error from a variety of sources. An error may arise from a transposition of an entry into either account. For example, an entry for £1,234 may be recorded in either the cash book or bank statement as £1,324. Another source of error may arise from the incorrect posting of entries. For example, an entry is recorded as a debit entry rather than a credit entry in the cash book or bank statement.

Test yourself 8.3

a) **What is a bank reconciliation?**

b) **Why is a bank reconciliation required?**

Worked example 8.3

The balance on Bluetown Transport Ltd's bank statement at 30 June 20X4 was £3,750 overdrawn. The company's cash book at the same date had a debit balance of £16,200. A comparison between the cash book and the bank statement revealed the following differences.

a) Cheques to the value of £1,500 had been entered in the cash book but had not yet appeared in the bank statement.

b) £25,000 deposited at the bank on 30 June 20X4 was entered in the cash book but not on the bank statement.

c) Bank charges of £450 had not yet been entered in the cash book.

d) A customer's payment of £4,000 had been made direct to the bank and no entry had yet been made in the cash book.

Update the cash book and reconcile the revised cash book with the balance on the bank statement.

Answer

The updated cash book is as follows:

Cash book				
Date	**Details**	**Dr**	**Cr**	**Balance**
30 Jun 20X4	Balance b/d	16,200		16,200
30 Jun 20X4	Bank charges		450	15,750
30 Jun 20X4	Sales ledger	4,000		19,750
30 Jun 20X4	Balance c/d			19,750

Note: b/d = brought down; c/d = carried down

The cash book had to be updated for the last two transactions because they were entered into the bank statement but they were not recorded in the cash book.

Bank reconciliation
30 June 20X4

Method 1

	£	**£**
Balance per cash book		19,750
Plus		
Uncleared cheque	1,500	1,500
		21,250
Less		
Bank lodgement not on bank statement	25,000	25,000
Balance as per bank statement 30 June 20X4		(3,750)

Or

Bank reconciliation
30 June 20X4

Method 2

	£	£
Balance as per bank statement		(3,750)
Plus		
Bank lodgement not on bank statement	25,000	25,000
		21,250
Less		
Uncleared cheque	1,500	1,500
Revised cash book balance		19,750

The reconciliation of the cash book and bank statement has to account for the two transactions already entered in the cash book but not appearing on the bank statement.

4. Control accounts

control account
An account that provides an arithmetic check of a ledger.

A **control account** is a trial balance for the debtor accounts and the sales account. The transactions in each debtor account and each creditor account are totalled and entered in the sales ledger control account or purchase ledger control account. The sales ledger control account is also known as the 'debtors control account'. Similarly, the purchase ledger control account is also known as the 'creditors control account'. The extensive use of computerised accounting systems in business may result in a separate control account no longer being generated, because the accounting systems can readily produce the individual debtor and creditor accounts plus the total balances for the debtor and creditor accounts.

In summary, a control account is an account that checks the arithmetic accuracy of a ledger, primarily the debtors and creditors, resulting in the terms 'sales ledger control account' and 'purchase ledger control account'.

4.1 The purpose of control accounts

The primary reason for control accounts is the arithmetic check on accuracy that they provide. This is similar to the trial balance discussed earlier in this chapter. However, unlike the trial balance, the control accounts are usually incorporated as part of the double-entry system.

The accuracy checks performed by the control accounts are as follows.

1. The sales ledger control account balance equals the sum of the total balances from the individual debtor accounts.
2. The purchase ledger control account balance equals the sum of the total balances from the individual creditor accounts.

The accuracy check is very important in the double-entry system, because posting errors can easily be made and can go undetected within the recording process. In addition, as seen in the case of the trial balance, errors may arise from a variety of sources.

Control accounts can make it easier to locate an error within the sales or purchase ledgers, especially when a control account is produced on a frequent basis. An error may be located by a comparative review of the control account and the individual sales or purchase ledger balances between reporting periods. The frequent preparation of control accounts enables a business to identify and locate errors much earlier than once a year, when the annual accounts are produced.

Fraudulent activities can be deterred or made more difficult through the operation of a control account. The perpetrator of the fraud would need to avoid the attention and security of the officer with the responsibility for the control account. However, a control account cannot prevent cooperation in crime between a perpetrator of fraud and the officer responsible for the control account.

The existence of a control account provides an internal control within the accounting system, if a business operates a system of segregation of duties in its bookkeeping system. The preparation and responsibility for the control account would be the responsibility of a different officer from the ones responsible for the individual sales and purchases accounts.

Management can receive more timely information to make decisions where a business has control accounts within their double-entry system. Management will no longer have to extract the balances from the individual debtor and creditor accounts, because the totals from the sales and purchase ledger control accounts will equal the total of the debtors and creditors balances.

4.2 Sales ledger control account

A **sales ledger control account** or a debtors ledger control account is a nominal ledger account that records the totals of entries made to the individual debtors ledger from the sales daybook, the sales return daybook and the cash book receipts. The sales ledger control account should always equal the total of the individual debtors ledger. Any differences should be examined to identify their sources and return the accounts to a state of balance.

sales ledger control account
A ledger control account that records the totals of entries in the individual debtors ledger. This is also known as the debtors ledger control account.

Worked example 8.4

On 31 July 20X4, Alphabet Co had extracted the following balances from their three accounts that made up their sales ledger:

July sales	£18,660
Sales returns	£4,270
Discounts allowed	£475
Cheques received	£24,500
1 July bal b/d	£18,660
Bad debts written off	£750

D Best				
Date	**Description**	**Dr**	**Cr**	**Balance**
1 Jul 20X4	Bal	4,980		4,980
3 Jul 20X4	Sales	6,775		11,755
4 Jul 20X4	Sales	3,420		15,175
4 Jul 20X4	Discount allowed		350	14,825
26 Jul 20X4	Bank		10,000	4,825
31 Jul 20X4	Balance			4,825

N Hope				
Date	**Description**	**Dr**	**Cr**	**Balance**
1 Jul 20X4	Bal	5,785		5,785
11 Jul 20X4	Sales	3,420		9,205
19 Jul 20X4	Sales returns		1,150	8,055
21 Jul 20X4	Bank		2,850	5,205
28 Jul 20X4	Sales	5,635		10,840
30 Jul 20X4	Bad debts		750	10,090
31 Jul 20X4	Balance			10,090

L Voucher				
Date	**Description**	**Dr**	**Cr**	**Balance**
1 Jul 20X4	Bal	7,895		7,895
8 Jul 20X4	Sales	12,555		20,450
8 Jul 20X4	Discount allowed		125	20,325
17 Jul 20X4	Bank		11,650	8,675
24 Jul 20X4	Sales	7,750		16,425
31 Jul 20X4	Sales returns		3,120	13,305
31 Jul 20X4	Balance			13,305

Prepare the sales ledger control account as at 31 July 20X4 and determine the closing balance.

Answer

The sales ledger control account for 31 July 20X4 is as follows:

Sales ledger control				
Date	**Description**	**Dr**	**Cr**	**Balance**
31 Jul 20X4	Bal	18,660		18,660
31 Jul 20X4	July sales	39,555		58,215
31 Jul 20X4	Sales returns		4,270	53,945
31 Jul 20X4	Bank		24,500	29,445
31 Jul 20X4	Discount allowed		475	28,970
31 Jul 20X4	Bad debts		750	28,220
31 Jul 20X4	Balance			28,220

It is important to note that the closing balance on 31 July 20X4 (£28,220) is not a mathematical deduction from the sales ledger control account. The balance is the sum of the closing balance from each of the individual accounts that constitute the sales ledger: £28,220 = 4,825 + 10,090 + 13,305.

This is not a surprise because the sales ledger control account records the totals of entries made to the individual debtors ledger accounts.

4.3 Purchase ledger control account

purchase ledger control account
A ledger control account that records the totals of entries in the individual creditors' ledger. This is also known as the creditors control account.

A **purchase ledger control account** or a creditors ledger control account is a nominal ledger account that records the totals of entries made to the individual creditors ledger from the purchase daybook, the purchases returns daybook and the cash payments. The purchases ledger control account should always equal the total of the individual creditors ledger. Any differences should be examined to identify their source and return the accounts to a state of balance.

Worked example 8.5

On 31 July 20X4, Alphabet Co had extracted the following balances from their three accounts that made up their purchase ledger:

1 July bal b/d	£9,115
July purchases	£17,430
Purchase returns	£4,830
Discounts received	£950
Payments made in July	£12,710

El Belle				
Date	**Description**	**Dr**	**Cr**	**Balance**
1 Jul 20X4	Balance		5,665	5,665
3 Jul 20X4	Purchases		3,330	8,995
4 Jul 20X4	Bank	3,420		5,575
4 Jul 20X4	Discount received	550		5,025
26 Jul 20X4	Purchase returns	1,275		3,750
31 Jul 20X4	Balance			3,750

B Goode				
Date	**Description**	**Dr**	**Cr**	**Balance**
1 Jul 20X4	Balance		2,350	2,350
2 Jul 20X4	Purchase returns	980		1,370
10 Jul 20X4	Purchase		3,500	4,870
28 Jul 20X4	Bank	2,895		1,975
31 Jul 20X4	Balance			1,975

S Dayes				
Date	**Description**	**Dr**	**Cr**	**Balance**
1 Jul 20X4	Balance		1,100	1,100
3 Jul 20X4	Bank	875		225
16 Jul 20X4	Purchases		4,050	4,275
16 Jul 20X4	Discount received	400		3,875
22 Jul 20X4	Purchases		6,550	10,425
28 Jul 20X4	Bank	5,520		4,905
29 Jul 20X4	Purchase returns	2,575		2,330
31 Jul 20X4	Balance			2,330

Prepare the purchase ledger control account as at 31 July 20X4 and determine the closing balance.

Answer

The purchase ledger control account for 31 July 20X4 is as follows:

Purchase ledger control				
Date	**Description**	**Dr**	**Cr**	**Balance**
31 Jul 20X4	Bal		9,115	9,115
31 Jul 20X4	Purchases		17,430	26,545
31 Jul 20X4	Bank	12,710		13,835
31 Jul 20X4	Discount received	950		12,885
31 Jul 20X4	Purchase returns	4,830		8,055
31 Jul 20X4	Balance			8,055

The entries found in the sales and purchase ledger control account are shown in Table 8.1.

Table 8.1: The elements of a sales and purchase ledger control account

Sales (debtor) control	
Dr	**Cr**
Opening balance	Cash received from debtors
Sales for the period	Sales return
	Discount allowed
	Bad debts

Purchase (creditors) control	
Dr	**Cr**
Purchase returns	Opening balance
Discount received	Credit purchases
Payment to creditors	

Test yourself 8.4

On 31 January 20X4, ENO Enterprises had the following balances on their sales and purchase ledger control accounts:

Sales ledger	**Dr £158,258**
Purchase ledger	**Cr £58,389**

The following is a summary of the transactions for 31 January 20X4.

	£
Sales on credit	**274,210**
Sales returns	**750**
Purchases on credit	**42,910**
Purchase returns	**1,072**
Cash received from debtors	**281,328**
Cash paid to creditors	**49,306**
Discounts received	**502**
Discounts allowed	**1,327**
Bad debts written off	**350**

a) Prepare the sales ledger control account as at 31 January 20X4.

b) Prepare the purchase ledger control account as at 31 January 20X4.

Chapter summary

- The trial balance is a list of balances on the accounts included in the ledger. The balances show the period end position on each account. For example, it will show how much customers owe a business, how much the business owes its suppliers or how much cash it has at the bank. The trial balance totals should be equal, as each transaction is recorded throughout the accounting period by at least two accounting entries of equal value.
- The trial balance is only an arithmetic check and will not detect every error in the double-entry system.

- A balanced trial balance does not indicate that the nominal ledger is free from any errors.
- A bank reconciliation statement is prepared to explain the differences between the balance on the cash book and the bank statement.
- The differences between the cash book and bank statement may arise for wholly legitimate and acceptable reasons.
- The cash book should always be written up before a bank reconciliation statement is prepared.
- A bank reconciliation statement can be prepared in two different ways but it will always provide the same explanations.
- Control accounts are usually prepared at the end of each month or accounting period, and provide an arithmetic check of the individual accounts.
- Sales ledger control accounts consist of balances drawn from the individual debtor accounts.
- Purchase ledger control accounts consist of balances drawn from the individual creditor accounts.
- Discrepancies between the control accounts and the feeder individual ledgers should be examined to identify the reason for the difference and corrected accordingly.

Test yourself answers

Test yourself 8.1

a) A trial balance is a list of the ledger account balances at one point in time. The trial balance lists the ledger accounts and their respective debit or credit balance. It is just an arithmetical check of the ledger balances, drawn up in two columns: debits and credits. This is important to note, because a trial balance may not be correct even if the total debits equal the total credits.

b) True. The sum of the debits of a trial balance is always equal to the sum of the credits.

c) False. A trial balance is not part of the double-entry bookkeeping system.

d) True. Although a trial balance is customarily drawn up at the end of an accounting period, it is possible to draw up a trial balance as frequently as required by an entity, therefore a trial balance can be drawn up on a weekly basis.

Test yourself 8.2

a) C – Commission

b) B – Transposition

c) An error of reversal of entry occurs when a transaction is entered in the correct accounts but each item has been entered on the wrong side of each account. For example, see section 2.4.

d) An error of principle arises when a transaction has been posted to the wrong type of account. For example, on 3 July 20X4, £4,125 was paid to FG Insurance Co, but the bookkeeper entered the payment as a debit in the administration account.

An error of compensation occurs when an error on one side of the ledger is wholly compensated by an error of equal value on the other side of the ledger. For example, on 6 July 20X4, the bookkeeper incorrectly overstated and entered a sales invoice and purchase invoice by £450.

Test yourself 8.3

a) A bank reconciliation is the process whereby the bank statement is initially compared with the cash book and any differences between the two statements are identified. Explanations are provided for any identified differences, such that the two are in equilibrium at the end of the process.

b) A bank reconciliation is required for three general reasons:

i) entries found on the bank statement only;

ii) entries found in the cash book only; and

iii) errors in the cash book and/or the bank statement.

Test yourself 8.4

a)

Sales ledger account				
Date	**Description**	**Dr**	**Cr**	**Balance**
31 January 20X4	Opening balance	158,258		158,258
31 January 20X4	Credit sales	274,210		432,468
31 January 20X4	Cash received from debtors		281,328	151,140
31 January 20X4	Sales returns		750	150,390
31 January 20X4	Discounts allowed		1,327	149,063
31 January 20X4	Bad debts written off		350	148,713
31 January 20X4	Closing balance			148,713

b)

Purchases ledger account				
Date	**Description**	**Dr**	**Cr**	**Balance**
31 January 20X4	Opening balance		58,389	58,389
31 January 20X4	Purchase returns	1,072		57,317
31 January 20X4	Purchases on credit		42,910	100,227
31 January 20X4	Cash paid to creditors	49,306		50,921
31 January 20X4	Discounts received	502		50,419
31 January 20X4	Closing balance			50,419

Part four

Chapter 9
Preparing financial statements: sole trader

Chapter 10
Preparing financial statements: limited companies and not-for-profit organisations

Chapter 11
Interpretation of financial statements

Reporting and analysing financial information

Overview

The final Part of this book integrates all the elements from the previous three sections and demonstrates which financial statements are constructed for different organisations. The construction process begins with the trial balance and Chapter 9 demonstrates the stages and ordering of the process to ensure the outcome is meaningful for the needs of users and provides a true reflection of the performance of the organisation.

The comparative financial statements for the different organisations are explored in Chapter 10 to highlight the similarities and differences. Chapter 11 completes the accounting journey with the use of accounting ratios to provide further meaning and interpretation of the financial performance of organisations to allow users to make reliable decisions. This completes the circle from business transactions to financial statements to undertaking further decisions and activity.

Learning outcomes

At the end of this Part, students will be able to:

- know how to prepare financial statements for a sole trader
- understand the format of financial statements of limited and public limited companies
- know how to prepare financial statements for not-for-profit organisations
- be able to interpret financial statements.

Chapter nine
Preparing financial statements: sole trader

List of topics

1. The trial balance
2. Preparing a sole trader's profit and loss account
3. Accounting for returns, carriages and discounts
4. Preparing a sole trader's balance sheet
5. Year-end adjustments

Introduction

This chapter consolidates much of the coverage of Part 2, bringing together the content and purpose of financial statements for a sole trader. The chapter explains how financial statements are constructed from a trial balance and demonstrates how the trial balance will have to allow for year-end adjustments, including cost of goods sold, accruals, prepayments, depreciation, bad debts and provision for doubtful debts. It is useful to classify the items in the trial balance in terms of those that can be identified as profit and loss account items (revenues and expenses), and balance sheet items (assets, liabilities and capital). The chapter explains how to construct a profit and loss account and identify the gross profit and the net profit. Balance sheets are also constructed and list fixed assets, current assets, current liabilities and long-term liabilities. The remainder of the balance sheet focuses on the capital of the owner.

1. The trial balance

Before the annual financial statements are prepared, a trial balance is drawn up from the nominal ledger. This is simply a list of all the nominal ledger balances. For example, if we look at the creditors account for a business, the balance will be calculated by taking the total of invoices received from suppliers and deducting from this figure the total of the credit notes for purchase returns plus the total cash paid by suppliers. The balance represents the liability of the business to the supplier (i.e. money owed).

As we saw in Chapter 5, if the balances comply with the rules of double-entry bookkeeping, the trial balance totals should be equal because each transaction has been recorded throughout the accounting period by at least two accounting entries of equal value.

Worked example 9.1

J Brown

Trial balance as at 30 June 20X4

	Dr	**Cr**
	£	**£**
Purchases	2,503,433	
Sales		3,891,079
Sales returns	150,628	
Purchase returns		16,716
Discounts allowed	16,132	
Discounts received		4,865
Salaries	452,712	
Heating	18,054	
Postage, printing and stationery	38,736	
Rent	280,000	
Fixed assets		
Plant and machinery	42,918	
Fixture and fittings	73,620	
Trade debtors	916,250	
Trade creditors		397,442
Bank	62,781	
Petty cash	75,670	
Drawings	72,850	
Profits b/f		23,682
Long-term loan		320,000
Capital b/f		50,000
	4,703,784	4,703,784

drawings
Monies or goods taken out of the business by a sole trader for private use.

Students should be familiar by now with all the items in the trial balance in Worked example 9.1 except for drawings and profit brought forward (b/f) from previous years. **Drawings** represent monies or goods taken out of the business by the owner. These monies are for the owner's private use and are not expenses of the business, so they are never recorded in the profit and loss account. Drawings represent a reduction in the funds the owner has invested in the business; they are a reduction of the owner's capital and so are recorded in the balance sheet. Profits brought forward from previous years represent the profits retained in the business; they are also called retained profits or reserves.

The trial balance is used as a basis for the preparation of the financial accounts.

Test yourself 9.1

The following ledger balances have been extracted from Cherry Bell's business for the year ending 31 December 20X4.

	£
Sales	**70,000**
Purchases	**26,000**
Rent	**8,000**
Sundry expenses	**7,000**
Loan interest	**2,000**
Debtors	**2,000**
Cash	**12,000**
Buildings	**12,000**
Fixtures	**36,000**
Loan	**12,000**
Profits b/f	**8,000**
Creditors	**3,000**
Drawings	**?**
Capital	**20,000**
Total	**218,000**

a) **Produce the trial balance for Cherry's business for the year ending 31 December 20X4 and determine her level of drawings.**

b) **Explain the term 'drawings' and where it appears in the financial statements.**

2. Preparing a sole trader's profit and loss account

The starting point in producing the profit and loss account is the trial balance. Assuming there are no year-end adjustments, the first step is to decide whether items in the trial balance should be included in the profit and loss account or the balance sheet. You will recall from Chapter 4 that revenues and expenses are profit and loss items, while assets, capital and liabilities are balance sheet items. Thus we can classify the trial balance items as shown in Worked example 9.2. This trial balance lists all the items very neatly in terms of grouping profit and loss and balance sheet together. In reality, the trial balance items are likely to be mixed up, so you must be confident that you can classify each item as to which financial statement it is entered in.

Worked example 9.2

J Brown

Trial balance as at 30 June 20X4

	Dr	**Cr**	**Profit and loss**	**Balance sheet**
	£	**£**	**£**	**£**
Purchases	2,503,433		2,503,433	
Sales		3,891,079	3,891,079	
Sales returns	150,628		150,628	
Purchase returns		16,716	16,716	
Discounts allowed	16,132		16,132	
Discounts received		4,865	4,865	
Salaries	452,712		452,712	
Heating	18,054		18,054	
Postage, printing and stationery	38,736		38,736	
Rent	280,000		280,000	
Fixed assets				
Plant and machinery	42,918			42,918
Fixture and fittings	73,620			73,620
Trade debtors	916,250			916,250
Trade creditors		397,442		397,442
Bank	62,781			62,781
Petty cash	75,670			75,670
Drawings	72,850			72,850
Profits b/f		23,682		23,682
Long-term loan		320,000		320,000
Capital b/f		50,000		50,000
	4,703,784	4,703,784		

The profit and loss account of a sole trader consists of two elements: trading account and profit and loss account, such that it is known as a trading profit and loss account. A trading account is prepared to reflect the sales less the costs of sales, excluding any other business costs. The output from the trading account is the gross profit.

A profit and loss account starts with the gross profit, generated by the trading account, and deducts all the other costs of running the business. A profit and loss account shows the business owner and the users of the account the net profit for the year. The trading profit and loss account based upon the trial balance from Worked example 9.1 is shown in Worked example 9.3.

Worked example 9.3

J Brown

Trading profit and loss account

For the year ending 30 June 20X4

	£	£
Sales		3,891,079
Less sales returns		150,628
		3,740,451
Less cost of goods		
Opening stock	0	
Add purchases	2,503,433	
Add carriage inwards	0	
	2,503,433	
Less purchase returns	16,716	
Less closing stock		2,486,717
Gross profit		1,253,734
Less expenses		
Salaries	452,712	
Heating	18,054	
Printing, postage and stationery	38,736	
Rent	280,000	
Discounts allowed	16,132	805,634
		448,100
Add income		
Discounts received	4,865	4,865
Net profit		452,965

Notes

1. **Sales represent the revenue from sales during the year.**
2. **Gross profit represents sales revenue less cost of sales.**
3. **Net profit is gross profit minus the expenses of running the business.**

3. Accounting for returns, carriages and discounts

When preparing a trading profit and loss account for a sole trader, dependent upon the business and its management, six adjustments may be required:

1. purchase returns;
2. sales returns;
3. carriage inwards;
4. carriage outwards;
5. discounts allowed; and
6. discounts received.

The accounting for these items are shown in Table 9.1.

Table 9.1: Accounting for returns, carriages and discounts

Item	Trading account	Profit and loss account
1. Purchase returns	A deduction from purchases which forms part of the cost of sales	
2. Sales returns	A deduction from sales, shown after sales in the trading account	
3. Carriage inwards	An addition to purchases which forms part of the cost of sales	
4. Carriage outwards		An expense in the profit and loss account
5. Discounts allowed		An expense in the profit and loss account
6. Discounts received	An income shown separately as an addition to gross profit	An income shown separately as an addition to gross profit or after the expenses.

3.1 Purchase returns

Purchase returns, as examined in Chapter 4, are the return of previously purchased items of stock to the supplier. To account for a purchase return, it is always shown as a deduction from the purchases, in the trading account.

3.2 Sales returns

Similar to purchase returns, sales returns are items previously sold by a business, but returned by the purchaser. To account for a sales return, it is always shown as a deduction after the sales figure in the trading account.

3.3 Carriage inwards

When goods are purchased from a supplier, the cost of transporting the goods from the supplier is known as the carriage inwards. This cost arises from the purchases of goods and is therefore charged to the trading account as part of the cost of sales.

3.4 Carriage outwards

Carriage outwards is the expense incurred by a business when distributing or transporting goods to a purchaser. The expenses are not part of the sales or selling price and as such are always shown as an expense in the profit and loss account.

3.5 Discounts allowed

When a business offers a credit purchaser a discount for early settlement, the discount granted is a discount allowed. The consequence of a discount allowed results in the business receiving a reduced amount for a sale. Although the sales revenue is reduced, a discount allowed is never charged to the trading account. Discounts allowed are always charged as a separate expense to the profit and loss account.

3.6 Discounts received

A discount received is the opposite of a discount allowed. When a business pays its account early and pays a reduced amount, the difference between the amount paid and the price on the original invoice is the discount received. Consequently, the business has received an income arising from this early settlement.

The income arising from a discount received may be recorded in the trading account immediately after the gross profit. Alternatively the discount received may be shown as income after the deduction for expenses in the profit and loss account.

4. Preparing a sole trader's balance sheet

A balance sheet reflects the accounting equation (see Chapter 3). The traditional format of the balance sheet is in a columnar format in two sections. The upper section provides a breakdown of the assets and liabilities. The lower section consists of the capital or the financing of the business. The most important feature of a balance sheet and its adherence to the accounting equation is that the two sections are always equal. The following are the key headings in the order in which they are found on a sole trader's balance sheet:

- fixed assets;
- current assets;
- current liabilities;
- net current assets or working capital;
- long-term liabilities;
- net assets;
- capital; and
- owner's funds.

The balance sheet should identify a subtotal for each of the above key items.

working capital ratio
A ratio that compares the current assets against the current liabilities. Also known as the current ratio.

The term 'net current assets' is a key figure on a balance sheet as it represents the **working capital** of the business. This is usually defined as current assets (stocks, debtors and cash) less current liabilities (creditors). Thus working capital represents the net investment in short-term assets. Such assets are continually flowing into and out of the business, and are essential to the day-to-day operations of the business. The importance of working capital is discussed further in Chapter 11. For the present it is important to remember how it is calculated and shown on the balance sheet.

net assets
The excess of book value of assets over liabilities, including loan capital.

Total **net assets** (in this case, £453,797) is the figure obtained when a total is obtained by adding together the total fixed assets (£116,538) and the net current assets (£657,259) and deducting the long-term liabilities (£320,000). In effect, this figure represents the excess of the book value of all the assets of the business over the total external liabilities of the business.

The owner's funds is the total of the original capital invested by the owner in the business, plus any retained profits or reserves from previous years, plus this year's profits less any drawings made by the owner during the year.

The two totals – the owner's funds and total net assets – are equal; the balance sheet 'balances' for the same reasons explained in Chapter 3 on the accounting equation. Worked example 9.4 shows the balance sheet based upon the trial balance from Worked example 9.1 and the trading profit and loss account in Worked example 9.3.

Worked example 9.4

	£	£	£
Fixed assets			
Plant and machinery			42,918
Fixture and fittings			73,620
			116,538
Current assets			
Trade debtors	916,250		
Bank	62,781		
Cash	75,670	1,054,701	
Current liabilities			
Trade creditors	397,442	397,442	
Net current assets			657,259
Long-term liabilities			
Long-term loan			320,000
Net assets			453,797
Financed by			
Capital account b/f			50,000
Add profit b/f			23,682
			73,682
Add net profit			452,965
Less drawings			72,850
Owner's funds			453,797

The term 'net' is used in the balance sheet. This is the figure obtained if the total of one set of items is deducted from another set of items in the balance sheet. For example, net current assets (£657,259) is obtained by taking the total current assets (£1,054,701) and deducting the total current liabilities (£397,442).

Test yourself 9.2

The trial balance for PJ Hotspur as at 31 July 20X4 is shown below.

	Dr	Cr
	£	£
Sales		260,000
Sales returns	14,680	
Purchases	128,000	
Purchase returns		1,021
Debtors	15,350	
Creditors		10,514
Long-term loan		9,758
Bank overdraft		12,291
Office and factory rent	16,880	
Opening stock	5,112	
Motor vehicles at cost	20,376	
Accumulated depreciation as at 31 July 20X4		3,680
Furniture and fittings at cost	14,650	
Accumulated depreciation as at 31 July 20X4		2,560
Plant and machinery at cost	102,320	
Accumulated depreciation as at 31 July 20X4		10,480
Carriage in	384	
Carriage out	292	
Travelling expenses	1,755	
Administration	10,004	
Repairs	254	
Salaries	67,960	
Telephone	4,018	
Drawings	20,500	
Discounts allowed	4,588	
Capital		116,819
	427,123	427,123

Notes

1 The valuation of the closing stock at 31 July 20X4 was £4,550.

2 Provision for doubtful debts for the year is £800.

3 The annual depreciation charges are as follows:

Fixed asset	**£**
Motor vehicles	**3,339**
Plant and machinery	**6,888**
Furniture and fittings	**1,465**

a) **Prepare the profit and loss account for PJ Hotspur for the year ending 31 July 20X4.**

b) **Prepare the balance sheet for PJ Hotspur as at 31 July 20X4.**

5. Year-end adjustments

Chapter 6 outlined and explained the need to make adjustments to accounting the trial balance prior to the preparation of period-end financial statements. This is because it is extremely unusual for the detail in the accounting records to mirror exactly the financial activity undertaken by an organisation in a financial period. A simple reason will be the time-lag between when a business activity occurs and the physical recording of the transaction in the accounting records.

When a trial balance is produced, it is therefore simply a list of all the nominal ledger balances, and these balances are before the year-end adjustments are made. The balances need to be adjusted, where appropriate, so that the correct figures can be included in the profit and loss account and balance sheet.

A summary of the impact of the adjustments is provided in Table 9.2.

Table 9.2: Adjustments

Year-end adjustment	Definition	Impact on profit and loss account	Impact on the balance sheet
Stocks	Finished goods bought or manufactured for resale.	Cost of sales as calculated below is included. Opening stock + Purchases – Closing stock = Cost of sales	The closing stock is shown in the as a current asset.
Accruals (expenses owing)	The cash payment has been made after the benefit has been received.	The relevant expense figure is increased by the amount of the accrual.	Show the amount of the accrual as a current liability on the balance sheet.
Prepayments (payments in advance)	The cash payment has been made before the benefit has been received.	The relevant expense figure is decreased by the amount of the prepayment.	Show the amount of the prepayment as a current asset on the balance sheet.

Year-end adjustment	Definition	Impact on profit and loss account	Impact on the balance sheet
Bad debts	An actual debt which is considered not to be collectable.	At the end of the accounting period (year), the business will determine which debtors balances are not recoverable from the original debtor. This is the amount that is shown in the trial balance and is charged to the profit and loss account.	The non-recoverable debtors amount reported in the profit and loss account is deducted from the total debtors balance reported in the trial balance to enable the computation of closing debtors balance at the end of the accounting period.
Provision for doubtful debts	This is an estimate of the proportion of the year-end debtors that will not be paid.	At the end of the accounting period (year), the business will determine the actual sum or percentage of its debtors, which may not recoverable. After the first year of trading, the difference between the current year and previous year as shown in the trial balance is reported in the profit and loss account.	Last year's provision is removed and replaced by the provision for this year as calculated at the year-end. This is shown as a deduction from the debtors in the balance sheet.
Provision for depreciation	The internal charge a business makes for the use and deterioration of fixed assets.	This year's annual depreciation is charged as an expense.	The fixed assets are shown as follows: (Cost of fixed asset less Cumulative depreciation) Net book value.

An example of preparing a sole trader's financial statements is shown in Worked example 9.5.

Worked example 9.5

B Jones has extracted the following trial balance from his ledgers for the year ending 30 June 20X4.

	Dr	Cr
	£	£
Purchases	2,503,433	
Sales		3,891,079
Sales returns	150,628	
Purchase returns		16,716
Discounts allowed	16,132	

Discounts received		4,865
Salaries	452,712	
Heating	18,054	
Postage, printing and stationery	38,736	
Rent	280,000	
Fixed assets at cost		
Plant and machinery	42,918	
Fixture and fittings	73,620	
Accumulated depreciation		
Plant and machinery b/f		28,178
Fixture and fittings b/f		44,173
Stock b/f	175,943	
Trade debtors	916,250	
Trade creditors		397,442
Bad debts written off	6,028	
Provision for doubtful debts b/f		34,500
Bank	62,781	
Petty cash	550	
Drawings	72,850	
Profits b/f		23,682
Long-term loan		320,000
Capital b/f		50,000
	4,810,635	4,810,635

Notes to the trial balance

- Stock at 30 June 20X4 was valued at £248,426.
- Accrued salaries at 30 June 20X4 were £22,430.
- The total rent balance includes £40,000 in respect of July and August 20X4.
- Depreciation on plant and machinery is calculated on a 30% reducing-balance basis.
- Fixtures and fittings are depreciated on a straight-line basis at 10% of cost.
- B Jones discovered that £4,250 due from Hyang stores is uncollectable, as the company went into liquidation on 9 June 20X4.

- The provision for doubtful debts on 30 June should be 4% of debtors.
  - a) Prepare B Jones's profit and loss account for the year ending 30 June 20X4.
  - b) Prepare B Jones's balance sheet as at 30 June 20X4.

Answers

a) B Jones
Trading profit and loss account for the year ending 30 June 20X4

	£	£	£
Sales			3,891,079
Less sales returns			150,628
			3,740,451
Less cost of goods			
Opening stock		175,943	
Add purchases	2,503,433		
Less purchase returns	16,716	2,486,717	
		2,662,660	
Less closing stock		248,426	
Cost of sales			2,414,234
Gross profit			1,326,217
Add discounts received			4,865
			1,331,082
Expenses			
Salaries	452,712		
Plus: accrued salaries	22,430	475,142	
Heating		18,054	
PPS		38,736	
Rent	280,000		
Less: prepaid rent	40,000	240,000	
Depreciation			
Plant and machinery (42,918 – 28,178) × 30%	4,422		
Fixture and fittings (73,620 × 10%)	7,362	11,784	

Bad debts written off (6,028 + 4,250)		10,278	
Provision for doubtful debts (916,250 – 4,250) × 4%	36,480		
Less provision b/f	34,500		
Increase in provision for doubtful debts		1,980	
Discounts allowed		16,132	
			812,106
			518,976

The notes that accompany the trial balance form part of the information required to produce the financial statements and therefore are incorporated into the preparation of the profit and loss account as follows.

Notes

- This provides the closing stock balance for the year to be applied to the trading account.
- Accrued salaries are added to the salaries and are charged to the profit and loss account.
- Prepaid rent of £40,000 is deducted from the total rent expense in the profit and loss account.
- Annual depreciation of plant and machinery is to be charged to the profit and loss account at a rate of 30% on the reducing-balance basis.
- Annual depreciation of fixtures and fittings is to be charged to the profit and loss account on a straight-line basis at 10% of cost.
- Trade debtors are to be reduced by the uncollectable amount of £4,250 and charged to the profit and loss account.
- The provision for doubtful debts must be adjusted to 4% of debtors. The adjustment required for B Jones was an increase in provision as the trade debtors had increased.

It is important for students to note the order of accounting for the provision for doubtful debts and bad debts and in the financial statements. Bad debt is always deducted from trade debtors before any provision for doubtful debts is made. The debtors balance must always reflect the collectable amount of debtors before any provision is made. If a provision for doubtful debts is made before the recognition of a change in bad debt, an under or over provision for doubtful debts will occur.

Worked example 9.5 (cont.)

b) B Jones

Balance sheet as at 30 June 20X4

	£	£	£
Fixed assets			
Plant and machinery	42,918	32,600	10,318
Fixtures and fittings	73,620	51,535	22,085
	116,538	84,135	32,403
Current assets			
Stock		248,426	
Debtors (916,250 – 4,250 – 36,480)		875,520	
Prepaid rent		40,000	
Bank		62,781	
Petty cash		550	
		1,227,277	
Current liabilities			
Creditors	397,442		
Accrued expenses	22,430	419,872	
Net current assets			807,405
Long-term liabilities			
Long-term loan			320,000
Net assets			519,808
Financed by			
Capital b/f			50,000
Profit b/f			23,682
			73,682
Add profit for the year			518,976
			592,658
Less drawings for the year			72,850
Owner's funds			519,808

The impacts of the notes that accompanied the trial balance on the balance sheet are set out below.

Notes

- This provides the closing stock balance in the balance sheet.
- Accrued salaries is an unpaid expense and is recorded under the current liabilities.
- The prepaid rent of £40,000 is a current asset and is recorded under current assets.
- The annual depreciation charge for plant and machinery is added to the accumulated depreciation b/f on the balance sheet.
- The annual depreciation charge for fixtures and fittings is added to the accumulated depreciation b/f on the balance sheet.
- Trade debtors is reduced by the uncollectable amount of £4,250 before any adjustment for a provision for doubtful debts.
- The increased provision for doubtful debts is deducted from the debtors balance after the bad debt has been written off.

Test yourself 9.3

Golda-Miller is the owner of a two-year-old design consultancy company. The accounting year-end is 31 August 20X4 and below is Golda-Miller's trial balance and notes detailing the adjustments required to prepare the year-end financial statements.

	Dr	Cr
	£	£
Sales		**177,250**
Sales returns	**15,198**	
Discounts allowed	**1,250**	
Discounts received		**795**
Salaries	**53,421**	
Office expenses	**32,739**	
Fixed assets at cost		
Computers	**15,600**	
Motor vehicles	**18,750**	
Accumulated depreciation		
Computers b/f		**9,100**
Motor vehicles b/f		**7,500**
Stock b/f		
Trade debtors	**65,500**	
Trade creditors		**18,453**

Bad debts written off	**1,950**	
Provision for doubtful debts b/f		**3,800**
Bank	**25,919**	
Drawings	**48,000**	
Profits b/f		
Long-term loan		**20,000**
Capital b/f		**41,429**
	278,327	**278,327**

Notes

- Accrued salaries at 31 August 20X4 were £475.
- Office expenses were prepaid by £2,682 at 31 August 20X4.
- The provision for doubtful debts at 31 August 20X4 should be reduced to £3,275.
- Depreciation of computers is on a reducing-balance basis at 35%. Motor vehicle is depreciated on a straight-line basis at 20% on cost.

a) Prepare Golda-Miller's profit and loss account for the year to 31 August 20X4.

b) Prepare Golda-Miller's balance sheet as at 31 August 20X4.

Chapter summary

- A trial balance is a list of ledger account balances at a specific date that provides an arithmetic check of the debit and credit balances.
- The trial balance total debits equal the total credits.
- The trial balance is used to assist in the preparation of the annual financial statements.
- A balancing trial balance does not always mean that the trial balance is error free.
- Adjustments to a trial balance are required to enable the preparation of the annual financial statements.
- Accrual adjustments have to be made for unpaid bills at the end of the accounting period by adding the expense to the item in the trading profit and loss account, and recording them as a current liability on the balance sheet.

- Prepayment adjustments have to be made for bills paid for in advance at the end of the accounting period by deducting the expenses from the items in the trading profit and loss account, and recording them as current assets on the balance sheet.
- Known uncollectable debts are bad debts and they must be deducted from the debtors balance at the end of the year to reflect the true debtors balance that is collectable.
- A provision for doubtful debts is made for any debt a business suspects it may not collect from the debtor.
- Drawings are withdrawals from a business by a sole trader and are always shown as a deduction from capital on the balance sheet.

Test yourself answers

Test yourself 9.1

a) **Trial balance for Cherry Bell's business as at 31 December 20X4**

	Dr	Cr
	£	£
Sales		70,000
Purchases	26,000	
Rent	8,000	
Sundry expenses	7,000	
Loan interest	2,000	
Debtors	2,000	
Cash	12,000	
Buildings	12,000	
Fixtures	36,000	
Loan		12,000
Profits b/f		8,000
Creditors		3,000
Drawings	X	
Capital		20,000
Total	113,000	113,000

Total Dr = £113,000
Total Dr less drawings = £105,000
Drawings = £8,000
Total Dr = £105,000 + £8,000 = Total Cr = £113,000

b) Drawings are the money or goods that a sole trader withdraws from their business for their personal use or consumption. A drawing represent a reduction of the owners' capital and is therefore reported on the balance sheet as a deduction from capital in the section of the balance sheet that represents the financing of the business which makes up the owner's funds.

Test yourself 9.2

a)

PJ Hotspur
Profit and loss account for the year ending 31 July 20X4

	£	£
Sales		260,000
Less: returns inwards		14,680
		245,320
Cost of goods sold		
Opening stock	5,112	
Purchases	128,000	
Carriage inwards	384	
	133,496	
Returns outwards	1,021	
	132,475	
Closing stock	4,550	127,925
Gross profit		117,395
Expenses		
Salaries and wages	67,960	
Rent	16,880	
Repairs	254	
Administration	10,004	
Telephone	4,018	
Carriage outwards	292	
Discounts allowed	4,588	
Travel	1,755	
Depreciation	11,692	
Provision for doubtful debts	800	118,243
Net profit		(848)

b) **PJ Hotspur**
Balance sheet as at the year ending 31 July 20X4

	Cost	Accum. depreciation	NBV
Fixed assets	£	£	£
Motor vehicle	20,376	7,019	13,357
Plant and machinery	102,320	17,368	84,952
Furniture and fittings	14,650	4,025	10,625
	137,346	28,412	108,934
Current assets			
Stock	4,550		
Debtors	14,550	19,100	
Current liabilities			
Creditors	10,514		
Overdraft	12,291	22,805	
Net current assets			(3,705)
Long-term liabilities			
Loan			9,758
Net assets			95,471
Financed by			
Capital at 1 August 20X3			116,819
Profit			(848)
			115,971
Less: Drawings			20,500
Capital 31 July 20X3			95,471

Test yourself 9.3

a) **Golda-Miller**
Profit and loss account for the year to 31 August 20X4

	£	£
Sales		177,250
Less sales returns		15,198
		162,052
Less expenses		
Salaries	53,896	
Office expenses	30,057	

Depreciation		
Computers	2,275	
Motor vehicle	3,750	
Bad debt	1,950	
Discounts allowed	1,250	93,178
		68,874
Add income		
Discounts received	795	
Provision for doubtful debts	525	1,320
Net profit		70,194

b)

Golda-Miller
Balance sheet as at 30 June 20X4

	£	£	£
Fixed assets	**Cost**	**Accum. depreciation**	**NBV**
Computers	15,600	11,375	4,225
Motor vehicle	18,750	11,250	7,500
	34,350	22,625	11,725
Current assets			
Stock			
Debtors	62,225		
Prepaid office expenses	2,682		
Bank	25,919		
		90,826	
Current liabilities			
Creditors	18,453		
Accrued expenses	475	18,928	
Net current assets			71,898
Long-term liabilities			
Long term loan			20,000
Net assets			63,623
Financed by			
Capital b/f			41,429
Profit b/f			0
			41,429

Add: profit for the year	70,194
	111,623
Less: drawings for the year	48,000
Owner's funds	63,623

Chapter ten

Preparing financial statements: limited companies and not-for-profit organisations

List of topics

1. Limited company financial statements
2. Public limited company financial statements
3. Preparing financial statements for not-for-profit organisations

Introduction

This chapter provides students with an overview of the structure of financial statements for limited companies and not-for-profit organisations. It will examine limited company financial statements and address the globalisation of business. Students will be introduced to financial statements prepared under International Financial Reporting Standards (IFRS) and UK Financial Reporting Standards (FRS) 102 and 105. The chapter concludes with an examination of not-for-profit organisations and looks at the content and structure of their financial statements.

1. Limited company financial statements

Students will not be required to produce full company financial statements under examination conditions, but they need to understand, be aware of the composition of, and be able to interpret company financial statements. The latter task will be discussed in Chapter 11. In addition, students need to be conversant with the structure and terminology of financial statements for public limited companies for international comparison.

A limited company is a legal entity separate from its owners, unlike a sole trader. The ownership and management of limited companies are usually separate, except in the case of small companies or family companies. Owners are shareholders and the management are the officers and employees of the company.

The content and presentation of company financial statements are usually governed by company law in the local jurisdictions.

1.1 Limited company profit and loss account

The profit and loss account for a company is less detailed than for a sole trader. It is no less informative, but is governed by the Companies Act 2006. The format commonly used for the presentation of limited company accounts is set out below.

Profit and loss account for a limited company for the year ending 31 December 20X4	
	£
Turnover	x
Cost of sales	(x)
Gross profit	x
Distribution costs	(x)
Administrative expenses	(x)
	x
Other operating income	x
Operating profit	x
Income from other investments	x
Profit before interest and tax	x
Net interest	(x)
Profit before tax	x
Tax on profit on ordinary activities	(x)
Post-tax profit	x
Dividends	(x)
Retained profit for the year	x

Figure 10.1: A sample profit and loss account for a limited company

A limited company trading account is identical to that of a sole trader, but thereafter differences arise. Distribution costs are the costs associated with the distribution of a company's goods/services to its customers or marketplace. The administration expenses are all the general operational expenses incurred in the daily operation of the company. Some examples include staff costs, office expenses, and printing, postage and stationery. The administration expenses may be regarded as the company's overheads. Other operating income is revenue income that arises from non-core activities, such as the disposal of a fixed asset.

For example, a railway company may earn income from the letting of properties that it owns. The rental income may be classified as other operating income because the company's core business is the operation of railways.

Income earned from savings and investments activities are separated and they are shown before taxable or pre-tax profit. Investment income is derived from a company's investment in securities or another company's shares. Net interest is the difference between bank interest receivable and payable.

After the deduction of corporation tax, a company is left with its post-tax profit. However, this is also the start of the appropriation account. This is the amount of profit that a company can choose to use at its discretion. The post-tax profit may be applied in four general ways:

1. reinvest for the future;
2. distribute to shareholders;
3. set aside provisions for known or unknown contingent liabilities; or
4. transfer to general reserves until a later date.

The residual after the appropriation is the profit retained for the year. This is a measure of how much a company has left after payment to every other stakeholder of their share of the turnover. The retained profit for the year is transferred to the revenue reserve on the balance sheet.

1.2 Limited company balance sheet

A limited company balance sheet is identical in structure to a sole trader's balance sheet except the use of the terms: creditors due within 12 months, creditors due over 12 months, and the lower section. Creditors due within 12 months has replaced current liabilities, and creditors due over 12 months has replaced long-term liabilities.

The lower section of a company balance sheet is the internal financing of the company. The main elements are the share capital, revenue reserves and capital reserves, as shown below.

The capital of a limited company is divided into shares and their owners are shareholders of the company. The share capital is the monetary value of the shares purchased and fully paid for by the shareholders. Revenue reserves are the accumulation of trading retained profit that a company may use for internal use or distribution to its shareholders in the future. Capital reserves are reserves that a company has accumulated from non-trading activity for use by the company but that are non-distributable to the shareholders. The shareholders' funds represent the capital owned by the shareholders, which is akin to the sole trader's funds in the balance sheet of the sole trader.

Balance sheet for a limited company at 31 December 20X4

	£	£	£
	Cost	**Accumulated depreciation**	**NBV**
Fixed assets			
Tangible	X	X	X
Intangible	X	X	X
	X	X	X
Current assets			
Inventory			
Trade debtors	X		
Prepayments			
Bank	X		
Cash	X		
	X		
Creditors due within 12 months			
Trade creditors	X		
Accurals	X		
	X		
Net current assets			X
Creditors due over 12 months			
Long-term loan			X
Net assets			XXX
Financed by			
Share capital			X
Revenue reserves			X
Capital reserves			X
Shareholders' funds			XXX

Figure 10.2: A sample balance sheet for a limited company

Test yourself 10.1

a) **Explain the difference between capital reserves and revenue reserves.**

b) **Explain the term 'retained profit'.**

c) **What is an appropriation account?**

1.3 Limited Company Financial Statements FRS 102

From January 2015, all UK non-listed companies (excluding small companies as defined by Companies Act 2006) were required to adopt Financial Reporting Standard (FRS) 102 when producing their financial statements. This was one of the first three new standards introduced to replace UK GAAP (Generally Accepted Accounting Practice) that sort to align UK financial reporting with the International Financial Reporting Standards (IFRS). The outcome of the adoption and application of FRS 102 was a change in the terminology of the financial statements. The profit and loss account became known as an 'income statement', and the balance sheet became known as a 'statement of financial position' in line with IFRS. FRS 102 permits the profit and loss account and statement of recognised gains and losses to be combined into one statement and this is called a 'statement of comprehensive income'. Examples of FRS 102 compliant financial statements are set out below.

Income statement for the year ending 31 December 20X4	
	£'000
Turnover	x
Cost of sales	x
Gross profit	x
Distribution costs	x
Administrative expenses	x
Operating profit (loss)	x
Profit (loss) on ordinary activities before interest	x
Interest receivable and similar income	x
Interest payable and similar charges	x
Other finance income	x
Profit (loss) on ordinary activities before taxation	x
Tax on profit on ordinary activities	x
Profit (loss) for the financial year	x

Figure 10.3: A sample income statement

Statement of other comprehensive income for the year ending 31 December 20X4	
Profit (loss) for the financial year	X
Unrealised surplus (deficit) on revaluation of freehold properties	X
Unrealised surplus on revaluation of investment properties	X
Total recognised gains (losses) relating to the year/ period	X

Figure 10.4: A sample statement of other comprehensive income

Statement of financial position as at 31 December 20X4			
	£	**£**	**£**
Fixed assets	**Cost**	**Accumulated depreciation**	**NBV**
Intangible assets	X	X	X
Property, plant and equipment	X	X	X
Investment property	X	X	X
Financial assets	X	X	X
	X	X	X
Current assets			
Inventories	X		
Debtors	X		
Financial assets	X		
Cash at bank and in hand	X		
	X		
Creditors			
Amounts falling due within one year	X		
Net current assets (liabilities)			X
Total assets less current liabilities			X
Creditors			
Amounts falling due after more than one year			
Long-term loan			X
Net assets			XXXX

Capital and reserves		
Called up share capital	x	
Share premium account	x	
Revaluation reserve	x	
Profit and loss account	x	
Shareholders' funds		xxxx

Figure 10.5: A sample statement of financial position

The financial statement terms used in the UK are derived from the Companies Act 2006 and therefore it is likely that for the foreseeable future, some companies will maintain the traditional names of 'profit and loss account' and 'balance sheet'. This lack of enforced changeover is further supported by FRS 102 paragraph 3.22, which states: 'an entity may use titles for the financial statements other than those used in this FRS as long as they are not misleading.'

1.4 Limited Company Financial Statements FRS 105

From January 2016, all UK micro entities are required to adopt Financial Reporting Standard (FRS) 105 when producing their financial statements. This was the latest UK FRS introduced to replace the former UK GAAP (Generally Accepted Accounting Practice) and align UK financial reporting with the International Financial Reporting Standards (IFRS).

An entity is deemed to be a micro entity if it satisfies at least two of the following three requirements in relation to a financial year:

1. Turnover: Not more than £632,000 (pro-rated appropriately where an entity's year is shorter or longer than a calendar year);
2. Balance sheet total (i.e. gross assets): Not more than £316,000; and
3. Average number of employees: Not more than 10.

In addition, an entity must satisfy at least two of the above conditions in two consecutive years to qualify as a micro-entity, and once qualified, must exceed at least two of these limits for two consecutive years to cease to qualify. Excluded from being classified as a micro entity are charitable companies and parent companies that are required or choose to prepare consolidated financial statements. There were amendments to FRS 105 in May 2016 to extend its scope to include eligible limited liability partnerships (LLPs) and qualifying partnerships. In December 2017 as part of the triennial review of FRS 102 the Financial Reporting Council made amendments to incorporate FRS 105 in the Republic of Ireland. Examples of FRS 105 compliant financial statements are set out below.

Format 1
Statement of financial position as at 31 December 20X4

	£'000	£'000
Called up share capital not paid	X	
Fixed assets	X	
Current assets	X	
Prepayments and accrued income	X	
Creditors: amounts falling due within one year	(X)	
Net current assets / (liabilities)		X/(X)
Total assets less current liabilities		X
Creditors: amounts falling due after more than one year		(X)
Provisions for liabilities		(X)
Accruals and deferred income		(X)
		X
Capital and reserves		X

Format 2
Statement of financial position as at 31 December 20X4

	£'000	£'000
Assets		
Called up share capital not paid		X
Fixed assets		X
Current assets		X
Prepayments and accrued income	X	X
Capital, Reserves and Liabilities		
Capital and reserves		X
Provisions for liabilities		X
Creditors		
Amounts falling due within one year	X	
Amounts falling due after one year	X	
		X
Accruals and deferred income		X
		X

Figure 10.6: The two formats of the statement of financial position

Income statement for the year ending 31 December 20X4		
		£'000
Turnover	X	
Other income		X
Cost of raw materials and consumables	(X)	
Staff costs		(X)
Depreciation and other amounts written off assets		(X)
Other charges		(X)
Tax		(X)
Profit or loss		X / (X)

Figure 10.7: A sample profit and loss account/ income statement

2. Public limited company financial statements

The content and structure of financial statements for public limited companies are determined by International Accounting Standard (IAS) 1, 'Presentation of Financial Statements'. IAS 1 prescribes the basis for the presentation of general-purpose financial statements, to ensure comparability with the entity's financial statements of previous periods and the financial statements of other entities.

A complete set of financial statements as per IAS 1 is as follows:

a) a statement of financial position as at the end of the period;

b) a statement of comprehensive income for the period;

c) a statement of changes in equity for the period;

d) a statement of cash flows for the period;

e) notes, comprising a summary of significant accounting policies and other explanatory information; and

f) a statement of financial position as at the beginning of the earliest comparative period when an entity applies an accounting policy retrospectively or makes a retrospective restatement of items in its financial statements, or when it reclassifies items in its financial statements.

However, the awareness of items (c), (d) and (e) above are outside the scope of this text and the Accounting syllabus.

2.1 Statement of comprehensive income

In accordance with IAS 1, the profit and loss account for a public limited company is entitled 'statement of comprehensive income'. However, for the purposes of the Accounting syllabus, students will not be required to produce financial statements compliant with IAS 1. Students will be required to interpret and explain the contents of the financial statements.

Statement of comprehensive income for the years ended 31 December 20X4

	20X4	**20X3**
	£'000	**£'000**
Revenue	550,000	470,000
Cost of sales	420,000	370,000
Gross profit	130,000	100,000
Distribution costs	12,000	8,000
Administrative expenses	24,000	18,000
Other expenses	9,000	6,000
Profit from operations	85,000	68,000
Interest payable	500	300
Profit before tax	84,500	67,700
Tax	25,350	20,310
Profit for the period from continuing operations	59,150	47,390
Discontinued operations		
Loss for the period from discontinued operations	6,200	4,500
Comprehensive income	52,950	42,890
Attributable to ordinary equity holders	42,360	34,312
Attributable to minority interest	10,590	8,578

Figure 10.8: A sample statement of comprehensive income

A format that covers most of the information that a student might expect to appear in an entity's income statement is shown in Figure 10.6. There are two presentations of the statement of comprehensive income. However, the statement of comprehensive income based on the function of the expense is the most popular approach and will therefore be used to meet the requirements of the Accounting examination.

IAS 1 also details additional information to be presented either on the face of the income statement or in the notes. Knowledge of these items is not required for the purpose of the Accounting examination.

2.2 Statement of financial position

The statement of financial position replaces the balance sheet for public limited companies. However, a statement of financial position is identical to a balance sheet except for some changes in terminology and the relocation of some items within the statement.

non-current assets
See fixed assets (page 34).

non-current liabilities
See long-term liabilities (page 33).

Current and **non-current assets**, and current and **non-current liabilities**, are presented as separate classifications on the face of the statement of financial position. These distinctions are required because how far into the future assets and liabilities are to be realised has clear implications for an assessment of the financial position and solvency of an entity. Any assets and liabilities not falling within the definition of 'current', as indicated below, are to be classified as non-current.

A current asset is one that is:

- expected to be realised, or is intended for sale or consumption, in the entity's normal operating cycle, is held primarily for trading purposes and is expected to be realised within 12 months of the balance sheet date; or
- cash or a cash equivalent asset.

A current liability is one that is:

- expected to be settled in the normal course of the entity's operating cycle; or
- due to be settled within 12 months of the balance sheet date.

A format that covers most of the information that one might expect to appear in a statement of financial position is shown in Figure 10.7.

IAS 1 also details information to be presented either on the face of the balance sheet or in the notes. Knowledge of these items is not required for the purpose of the Accounting examination.

Figure 10.9: A sample statement of financial position

Statement of financial position at 31 December		
	20X4	**20X3**
Assets	**£'000**	**£'000**
Non-current assets		
Property, plant and equipment	607,000	602,000
Accumulated depreciation	134,000	119,000
	473,000	483,000
Goodwill	11,000	11,000
Accumulated impairment	5,000	4,000
	6,000	7,000
Other intangible assets	13,000	9,000
Investments in associates	9,000	9,000

Available-for-sale investments	13,000	6,000
	35,000	24,000
Total non-current assets	514,000	514,000
Current assets		
Inventories	34,000	24,000
Trade receivables	24,000	18,000
Cash and cash equivalents	22,000	21,000
Total current assets	80,000	63,000
Total assets	594,000	577,000
Equity and liabilities		
Share capital	50,000	50,000
Other reserves	63,000	63,000
Retained earnings	225,000	172,050
	338,000	285,050
Minority interest	103,000	92,410
Total equity	441,000	377,460
Non-current liabilities		
Long-term borrowings	52,000	56,000
Deferred tax	11,000	9,000
Long-term provisions	5,000	5,000
Total non-current liabilities	68,000	70,000
Current liabilities		
Trade and other payables	13,000	26,540
Short-term borrowings	36,000	68,000
Current portion of long-term borrowings	6,000	6,000
Taxation	25,000	20,000
Short-term provisions	5,000	9,000
Total current liabilities	85,000	129,540
Total liabilities	153,000	199,540
Total equity and liabilities	594,000	577,000

Test yourself 10.2

a) **Outline the reason for the introduction of FRS 102.**

b) **Complete the missing entries labelled A–H in the following table.**

Sole trader	UK Limited Co (FRS 102)	Public limited company
Balance sheet	A	B
Profit and loss account	C	D
Stock	E	F
Trade debtors	G	H

2.3 Statutory Reporting of financial statements

Preparation of company financial statements is not the end of the annual reporting process. Financial statements have to submitted to two statutory bodies within the UK; The Registrar of Companies (England, Wales & Scotland) and HM Revenue and Customs (HMRC). The former is known operationally as Companies House. Each body has their own filing requirement and deadline date for limited companies.

All limited companies are required to file their annual financial statement at Companies House. Companies are required to file a signed copy of the financial statements prepared for its members. Small companies and micro entities may file abridged financial statements. The latter is a less detailed format of the full financial statement and excludes some balance sheet items. The deadline for the filing of company financial statements are determined by each company's accounting reference date (ARD). A private limited company must file their financial statements to Companies House within nine months of the company's ARD and a public limited company must file their financial statements within six months of its ARD.

Companies will incur a late payment penalty for late filing of their financial statements. This is shown in table 10.1 below

Table 10.1 Companies House penalties for late filing of filing financial statements

Late Period	Private Company	Public Company
Under 1 month	£150	£750
1 month < late < 3 months	£375	£1,500
3 months < late < 6 months	£750	£3,000
Over 6 months	£1,500	£7,500

Companies are also required to file their Financial statements with HMRC and akin to Companies House, the filing deadline date to HMRC is also determined by the company's ARD. Each company must file their financial statements to HMRC within 12 months of its ARD. Unlike Companies House, HMRC operates five classes of penalties as follows:

1. Failure to notify HMRC
2. Late filing
3. Late payment
4. Failure to keep records
5. Inaccuracies

3. Preparing financial statements for not-for-profit organisations

Many organisations do not receive their income from sales income and are not created to generate a profit. These **not-for-profit organisations** are established with an objective of being non-profit-making. The heading covers a multitude of bodies, including:

not-for-profit organisation
A non-commercial organisation that does not exist in order to make a profit and is unable to distribute any of its annual surplus to its members.

- central government departments;
- public corporations;
- local authorities;
- health authorities;
- charities and voluntary bodies – for example, Oxfam or Age Concern; and
- clubs and societies – for example, a local swimming club or an amateur dramatic group.

These bodies are set up to provide services without making a profit. This is not to say that such organisations are not involved in some trading activities, but making a profit is not the driving force of their activity. Depending on the nature, size and sources of funding of such bodies, their accounting records will vary. Many bodies maintain full accounting records, in which case the preparation of their accounts follow the normal process from trial balance to final accounts, making the necessary adjustments for accruals, prepayments and the like.

Some, like local authorities, universities and other government-funded bodies, follow accounting procedures that, although similar to those used in the private sector, also reflect the specialist nature of such bodies.

The accounting requirements of many of these bodies are determined by their legal form. For example, a UK charity has to comply with the UK Charities Act and produce accruals-based accounts. Contrast this with smaller not-for-profit organisations such as clubs and societies that are run so that their members can undertake activities such as swimming, rambling, chess or amateur dramatics. They are unlikely to draw up trading profit and loss accounts and balance sheets.

The nature and accounting arrangements of not-for-profit bodies are so diverse and specialised that they are beyond the scope of this book. However, we shall focus here on the accounts of clubs and societies, which will introduce receipts and payments accounts, and **income and expenditure accounts**.

income and expenditure account
An annual financial statement for a non-profit-making organisation that reflects the surplus or deficit made during the accounting period.

3.1 The income of clubs and societies

The sources of income for clubs and societies include:

- entrance fees or joining fees – entrance fees are charges made to new applicants on their admission as members;
- subscriptions – these are the annual amounts receivable from members;
- life membership fees – a member pays a lump sum in return for membership for the rest of their life;
- charges made to members for the use of club facilities; and/or
- surpluses from trading activities such as a licensed bar or car boot sale.

The accounts used to record the financial transactions of clubs and societies are known as receipts and payments accounts, or income and expenditure accounts.

3.2 The receipts and payments account

The receipts and payments account is a report of the cash transactions during a single financial period. It is used when it is not considered appropriate to distinguish between capital and revenue transactions or to include accruals. This means that there are no adjustments, including depreciation, doubtful debts, expenses owing, prepayments, etc.

In effect, the receipts and payments account is a summary of the cash transactions. The receipts and payments account records cash coming in (the receipts) and cash going out (the payments). The difference between the two sides represents the cash balance at the end of the accounting period. Worked example 10.1 shows a receipts and payments account.

Worked example 10.1

The Merry Players Amateur Dramatics Club

Receipts and payments account for the year ending 31 December 20X4		
Receipts	£	£
Bank balance at 1 January 20X4		5,236
Subscriptions received		4,740
Rent received		114
Total receipts		10,090
Payments		
Caretaker's wages	2,728	
Costume expenses	296	
Purchase of lighting	3,000	
Committee expenses	750	
Printing and stationery	436	
Total payments		7,210
Bank balance at 31 December 20X4		2,880

Review of receipts and payment account

Although relatively easy to produce, the receipts and payments account does not provide a comprehensive picture of the financial position of the club or society, for the following reasons.

1. There is no distinction between capital and revenue. In Worked example 10.1 above, the cash paid includes both the purchase price of a fixed asset and the wages paid to the caretaker.
2. Depreciation of fixed assets is not provided for; in the above example, the full cost of the lighting is recorded in one year's accounts.
3. Accruals and prepayments are not included, so members cannot determine whether the club has made a surplus or a deficit. For example, the members' subscriptions included as receipts do not make adjustments for any subscriptions that are outstanding or paid in advance.
4. The assets and liabilities of the club are not disclosed. In the above, the asset of cash is recorded at the beginning and end of the year, but no allowance is made for assets purchased in earlier years or creditors and debtors at the end of the year.
5. No balance sheet is produced.

These weaknesses can be illustrated by reference to Worked example 10.1. In short, the receipts and payments account is simply to be regarded as the cash summary.

3.3 The income and expenditure account

This is a financial statement for not-for-profit entities such as clubs, associations and societies. It shows the surplus/deficit, i.e. the surplus of income over expenditure or vice versa, for a period, and is drawn up on the same accruals basis as a profit and loss account.

Rather than using the term 'profit and loss account', the financial statement is normally called the 'income and expenditure account', to emphasise that the main object of a club is to provide a service to its members rather than to make a profit. For the same reason, the balance at the end of the income and expenditure account is the 'surplus of income over expenditure', or 'excess of expenditure over income' for the period, rather than 'profit' or 'loss'. The income and expenditure account is prepared following the same accounting rules as for trading profit and loss accounts.

The club will also produce a balance sheet in which the capital account may be called the accumulated fund. Any surplus for the year is added to the club fund account exactly as a profit would be added to the capital account in the balance sheet of a sole trader or small business.

The differences in the terminology used are shown in Table 10.2.

Table 10.2: Differences in terminology

Public listed company	Not-for-profit organisation
Statement of comprehensive income	Income and expenditure account
Profit before tax	Surplus of income over expenditure
Total equities and liabilities	Accumulated fund

Producing an income and expenditure account

The receipts and payments (or cash) account provides the basic information for producing the income and expenditure account. The receipts and payments account reveals when money was received or paid out. However, this does not give the organisation real information on its financial position, because payments may be received or made in advance or in arrears.

When an organisation owns assets and has liabilities, the receipts and payments account is not an informative way of presenting the annual accounts. Other than the cash received and paid out, it shows only cash balances and omits other assets and liabilities. The income and expenditure account records all the transactions during the period, whether or not money changed hands during this time – i.e. the accruals concept is applied. This will allow the organisation to see whether its capital has increased during the period. It also allows the organisation to produce a balance sheet.

For examination purposes, it is useful to know about the receipts and payments account because a question will often contain such a statement, along with other information, and ask for it to be converted into an income and expenditure account and balance sheet.

3.4 Subscription income

One of the major sources of income for clubs and societies are members' subscriptions. The process of working out the actual subscription income to be included in the income and expenditure account is complicated by the fact that subscriptions can be paid in advance or in arrears at both the beginning of the period and the end. It is important that students have their wits about them when they are working out the figure for subscriptions.

Students should remember that subscriptions owing at the beginning and end of the year are current assets of the organisation. In effect, the members whose subscriptions are outstanding are debtors of the club or society. On the other hand, subscriptions paid in advance at the beginning and end of the period are current liabilities of the club. In effect, the members who pay their subscriptions before they are due are creditors of the club or society.

Another point is that subscriptions in arrears may never be received. In accordance with the prudence concept (see Chapter 2), subscriptions in arrears should be reviewed regularly, and those that have been outstanding for a long time should be written off as irrecoverable. If this is not done, the organisation's assets will be overvalued. In practice, many clubs and societies follow the prudence concept fully and ignore subscriptions in arrears for final accounts purposes. The examination question should make clear exactly what the club's policy is in regard to such subscriptions. If in doubt, make an assumption and state it – for example, that all of the subscriptions in arrears will be collected and so included in the final accounts.

Calculating the subscription income for a period

To calculate the subscription income to be included in the income and expenditure account, students will have to allow for the fact that subscriptions can be in advance or in arrears at both the beginning of the period and the end. This can be allowed for by adjusting the actual cash received for subscriptions. This is done as follows:

	£
Cash received from members	X
Less (subscriptions in arrears at beginning of year)	(X)
Plus subscriptions in arrears at end of year	X
Plus subscriptions in advance at beginning of year	X
Less (subscriptions in advance at end of year)	(X)
Equals subscriptions to be included in income and expenditure account	XX

These adjustments are illustrated in Worked example 10.2.

Worked example 10.2

The South Bridge Golf and Country Club charges its members an annual subscription of £1,000, payable annually in advance. At 1 January 20X4, the club had received subscriptions in advance for the year for 13 members. Two members had failed to pay their subscription for the previous year at this date, but both did so early in 20X4. The total amount received from members during 20X4 was £396,000 at 31 December 20X4. Subscriptions received in advance for the next year amounted to £18,000, and three members failed to pay their 20X4 subscriptions. All three had promised to pay, and the committee had decided to prepare the club's accounts on the basis that they would, in fact, be received.

How much can be credited to the club's income and expenditure for subscriptions for the year 20X4?

Answer

		£
Cash received from members		396,000
Less subscriptions in arrears at beginning of year, i.e. relating to previous year	2 members @ £1,000	(2,000)
Plus subscriptions in arrears at end of year, i.e. due for 20X4 but not paid	3 members @ £1,000	3,000
Plus subscriptions in advance at beginning of year, i.e. relating to 20X4	13 members @ £1,000	13,000
Less subscriptions in advance at end of year, i.e. relating to following year	18 members @ £1,000	(18,000)
Subscriptions to be included in income and expenditure account for 20X4		392,000

3.5 Other income

If the club operates a bar or similar activity, it may be necessary to prepare a trading account to calculate the profit or loss arising on that activity.

For other one-off activities such as a Christmas dance or concert where the club has income, perhaps from sales of tickets, and related expenditure it is better to show the net result. This will clarify whether or not the activity covered its costs, rather than including the receipts along with the income and the costs among the other items of expenditure.

Worked example 10.3 illustrates the preparation and format of an income and expenditure account.

Worked example 10.3

The Hazlemere Sports and Social Club prepare its accounts to 31 December. The club's assets and liabilities as at 1 January 20X4 were as follows:

	£	£
Fixtures and fittings		68,000
Bar stocks		1,200
Rent prepaid		2,300
Balance at bank		2,200
		73,700
Less creditors		
Bar supplies	1,100	
Light and heat	500	1,600
Accumulated fund as at 1 January 20X4		72,100

The club secretary has prepared a summary of the club's receipts and payments for the year to 31 December 20X4:

Receipts	**£**	**Payments**	**£**
Bank balance at 1 January 20X4	2,200	Bar purchases	27,500
Members' subscriptions	32,000	Heat and light	2,600
Loan	20,000	Rent	10,000
Bar sales	44,000	Manager's wages	12,000
Christmas dance receipts	7,500	General expenses	8,500
Total receipts	105,700	New pool tables	7,500
		Christmas dance expenses	5,100
		Loan interest	2,000
		Bar person's wages	8,000
		Bar expenses	5,000
		Total payments	88,200
		Bank balance at 31 December 20X4	17,500
	105,700		105,700

The following information is also available:

1. At 31 December 20X4, rent prepaid was £3,000 and electricity outstanding was £600.
2. The bar stocks at 31 December 20X4 were valued at £1,400.
3. The club has decided to depreciate all fixed assets held at the year-end by 10%.
4. Subscriptions owing by members on 31 December 20X4 amounted to £4,550.

You are required to prepare the club's income and expenditure account for the year to 31 December 20X4 and a balance sheet as at that date. The club has asked that you prepare a separate account to show the profit or loss made by the bar.

Answer

A separate trading account to arrive at the profit from the bar is shown below. The profit is shown in the club's income and expenditure account. The separate trading account allows club members to see the financial results of operating the bar.

Hazlemere Sports and Social Club
Bar trading account for the year ending 31 December 20X4

	£	£	£
Bar sales			44,000
Bar stock at 1 January 20X4	1,200		
Add purchases (27,500 – 1100)*	26,400	27,600	
Less stock at 31 December 20X4	1,400		
Less cost of sales			26,200
Gross profit			17,800
Less bar person's wages	8,000		
Bar expenses	5,000		13,000
Net profit to income and expenditure account			4,800

*Note the purchases are reduced by the creditor for bar purchases unpaid at 1 January 20X4.

Hazlemere Sports and Social Club
Income and expenditure account for the year ending 31 December 20X4

	£	£
Income		
Subscriptions for 20X4 (32,000 + 4,550)		36,550
Profit from the bar		4,800
Christmas dance		
Receipts	7,500	
Less expenses	5,100	2,400
Total income		43,750
Expenditure		
Heat and light (2,600 – 500 + 600)	2,700	
Rent (10,000 + 2,300 – 3,000)	9,300	
Loan interest	2,000	
General expenses	8,500	
Depreciation (68,000 + 7,500) × 10%	7,550	
Manager's wages	12,000	42,050
Surplus of income over expenditure		1,700

Working notes to the income and expenditure account

1. The subscriptions of some members are arrears at the end of the year. The £4,550 has to be added to the subscriptions received to determine the subscription income for the year.
2. For one-off activities such as the Christmas dance where the club has income, perhaps from sales of tickets, and related expenditure, it is better to show the net result. This will clarify whether or not the activity covered its costs, rather than including the receipts along with the income and the costs among the other items of expenditure.
3. The heat and light figure of £2,600 represents the cash paid, but £500 was a creditor for the previous year while £600 is owing for electricity at the end of 20X4.
4. The rent figure of £10,000 has to be increased by the prepayment of £2,300 at the beginning of the year and reduced by the prepayment of £3,000 at the end of the year.
5. The depreciation is calculated at 10% on the fixed assets at the beginning of the year plus the fixed assets purchased during 20X4.

Hazlemere Sports and Social Club
Balance sheet as at 31 December 20X4

Fixed assets	**Cost**	**Accumulated depreciation**	**Net book value**
	£	**£**	**£**
Fixtures and fittings	75,500	7,550	67,950
Current assets			
Bar stocks	1,400		
Rent, prepaid	3,000		
Subscriptions owing	4,550		
Bank	17,500	26,450	
Less current liabilities			
Creditors – electricity		600	
Working capital			25,850
			93,800
Accumulated fund			
Balance at 1 January 20X4			72,100
Add surplus for year			1,700
			73,800
Loan			20,000
			93,800

Working notes to balance sheet

1. The prepaid rent is shown as a current asset.
2. The subscriptions owing by the members at the end of 20X4 are a current asset.
3. The electricity owing is a current liability.
4. The surplus for the year is added to the accumulated fund.

Test yourself 10.3

State whether the following statements are true or false.

a) Clubs and societies show their income in their profit and loss account.

b) Clubs and societies do not produce a balance sheet.

c) The main income source for clubs and societies comes from bar sales.

d) It is better to report the net result of sundry income from one-off club and societies activities.

Chapter summary

- The financial statements of limited companies and public limited companies are similar to a sole trader's financial statement.
- Public limited companies' financial statements must comply with IFRS.
- UK non-listed companies (excluding small companies as defined by Companies Act 2006) are required to comply with FRS 102 for financial reporting.
- The FRS 102 financial statements are an income statement and a statement of financial position.
- FRS 102 seeks to align UK financial reporting with IFRS.
- A statement of financial position and a statement of comprehensive income for the period are two of the five items required to comply with IAS 1.
- Not-for-profit organisations are not engaged in commercial trading and do not produce financial statements like commercial organisations.
- Not-for-profit organisations' financial statements consist of an income and expenditure account and a balance sheet.
- Not-for-profit organisations normally consist of an income and expenditure account, which corresponds to the profit and loss account of a trading concern, and a balance sheet.

Test yourself answers

Test yourself 10.1

a) Capital reserves are reserves that a company has accumulated from non-trading activity for use by the company but that are non-distributable to the shareholders. Revenue reserves are the accumulation of trading retained profit that a company may use for internal use or distribution to its shareholders in the future.

b) Retained profit is the profit that a company has at the end of the year after it has discharged all of its operating expenses, interest charges, tax liabilities and distribution to its shareholders.

c) An appropriation account shows the total funds available to a company after it has discharged all its operating expenses and tax liabilities. Secondly, an appropriation account also shows how these residual funds are distributed between shareholders and internal re-investment.

Test yourself 10.2

a) FRS 102 was introduced former UK GAAP and align UK financial reporting with IFRS.

b)

Sole trader	UK Limited Co (FRS 102)	Public limited company
Balance sheet	**A** Statement of financial position	**B** Statement of financial position
Profit and loss account	**C** Income statement	**D** Statement of comprehensive income
Stock	**E** Inventory	**F** Inventory
Trade debtors	**G** Debtors	**H** Trade receivables

Test yourself 10.3

a) False – Clubs and societies show their income in a receipts and payment account.

b) False – Clubs and societies do produce a balance sheet.

c) False – he main income source for clubs and societies comes from subscriptions.

d) True – It is better to report the net result of sundry income from one-off club and societies activities.

Chapter eleven
Interpretation of financial statements

List of topics

Introduction

This chapter discusses the use of accounting ratios to provide a framework to interpret the meaning of company financial statements; this will allow students to communicate the content of the financial statements to other users. The chapter identifies the key accounting ratios, how they are derived and their meaning to aid communication. Four classes of accounting ratios are examined throughout the chapter: profit margins, solvency, working capital management and gearing ratios. To complete the discussion of how to interpret financial statements using accounting ratios, the chapter concludes with an examination of the limitations of the accounting ratios.

1. Principles of ratio analysis

The financial statements published annually by companies are an important source of information for external users, and their form and content are carefully regulated with the intention of ensuring that they provide a helpful and reliable guide to corporate progress and user groups. The amount of useful information that can be gleaned from the income statement and balance sheet, however, is severely limited, even when a detailed breakdown of trading results is provided. For example, the income statement might show that purchases amount to £500 million, and the balance sheet might disclose trade creditors totalling £21 million, but it is impossible to assess whether these amounts, taken in isolation, are satisfactory or unreasonable.

Accounting ratios and ratio analysis have been developed to help translate the information contained in the accounts into a form that is more helpful and readily understandable to users of financial reports. The ratios do not appear in the financial statements, but are calculated from the contents of these.

Accounting ratios are calculated by expressing one figure as a ratio or percentage of another, with the objective of disclosing significant relationships and trends that are not immediately evident from the examination of individual balances appearing in the accounts. However, the ratio that results from a comparison of two figures possesses real significance only if an identifiable commercial relationship exists between the numerator and the denominator. For example, one would expect there to be a positive relationship between net profit and the level of sales. Assuming that each item sold produces a profit, one would expect a higher sales figure to produce more profit.

accounting ratios
The relationship between two or more items from the financial statements.

The significance of an accounting ratio is enhanced by comparison with some yardstick of corporate performance. There are three options available, namely comparison with:

1. results achieved during previous accounting periods by the same company (trend analysis);
2. results achieved by other companies (inter-firm comparisons); and
3. predetermined standards or budgets.

The advantage of making comparisons is that it enables users to benchmark a company's performance as good, average or poor in certain key areas relative to one of the three options identified above.

2. Profit margins

The knowledge of the numerical value of the annual profit is not particularly informative. What is of greater interest is the profit expressed as a relationship of another variable, such as sales.

2.1 Gross profit margin

The **gross profit margin** is the relationship between the gross profit and the sales, and it is expressed as follows:

gross profit margin
A ratio that reflects the gross profit as a percentage of the sales for a business.

$$\text{Gross profit margin} = \frac{\text{Gross profit}}{\text{Sales}} \times 100$$

The gross profit margin (GPM) indicates the amount of profit that a company generates per unit of sales. For example, a GPM of 25% informs the reader of the profit and loss account that for every £100 of sales, the company generates £25 of profit. The GPM measures the ability of a company to control its cost of goods in order to generate a profit. The higher the GPM, the more effective a company has been in controlling its cost of sales.

Changes in the GPM between periods may result from a change in:

- the sales price;
- the cost of sales; or
- the sales mix.

The GPM varies between companies and over time as productive capacity and operations change.

Company owners can learn from their GPM how the company has performed relative to previous years, relative to its own goals and targets, and relative to its competitors in the same sector. However, the GPM does not take into account the operating costs of a company; therefore it is somewhat limited as a measure of overall company performance.

2.2 Net profit margin

net profit margin
A ratio that reflects the net profit as a percentage of the sales for a business.

The **net profit margin** is calculated in different ways for sole traders and limited companies. For a sole trader, the simple measure of net profit margin is used as follows:

$$\text{Net profit margin} = \frac{\text{Net profit}}{\text{Sales}} \times 100$$

Whereas for a limited company the net profit margin, or (as it is more commonly termed) the operating profit margin, is as follows:

$$\text{Net profit margin} = \text{Operating profit margin} = \frac{\text{Operating profit}}{\text{Sales}} \times 100$$

The net profit margin is a measure of how well a company has used or combined its resources to generate a profit for the accounting period. The higher the net profit, the more effective the use that has been made of the company's resources. The difference between the net profit margin and gross profit margin is the expenses consumption margin. This is a measure of how much of the sales revenue has been consumed by the overheads of the company.

In a similar manner to the gross profit margin, the net profit margin is most useful when used as a comparison for a company rather than in isolation.

Test yourself 11.1

a) **To calculate the gross profit margin for a business, the business owner must express the gross profit as a percentage of which one of the following?**

A Cost of sales

B Net profit

C Purchases

D Sales

b) **During the year ending 30 June 20X4, the business cost of sales of £6,400 represented 40% of turnover. What was the annual gross profit?**

A £6,080

B £6,400

C £9,600

D £10,560

c) **The following is an extract from the books of Ivor Brain Construction for the year ending 31 January 20X4.**

	£
Turnover	**38,000**
Cost of sales	**23,000**
Operating expenses	**9,100**
Operating profit	**5,900**

What was the gross profit margin for the year?

A 65.22%

B 60.53%

C 39.47%

D 15.53%

3. Solvency

The **solvency** ratios are concerned with the ability of a business to meet its short-term debts or liabilities. There are two ratios in this class.

solvency
The ability of a business to pay its short-term debts as they become due and payable.

3.1 Current (working capital) ratio

The **current ratio** or working capital ratio is defined as the excess of current assets over current liabilities, and a surplus is normally interpreted as a reliable indication of the fact that a company is solvent. The current ratio is calculated as follows:

current ratio
See working capital ratio (see page 148).

$$\text{Current ratio} = \frac{\text{Current assets}}{\text{Current liabilities}} : 1$$

The purpose of the current ratio is to assess and measure the ability of a company to pay its current debts as they fall due. A general benchmark for the current ratio is 2:1. However, this should not be interpreted as a set standard for all companies. Any deviation from 2:1 should not be interpreted as signifying a better or worse outcome without further investigation or explanation.

The current ratio as a measure of solvency suffers from one limitation: its inclusion of inventories. To be solvent, a company needs to be able to convert its current assets into cash at short notice and with minimal cost. Unfortunately, inventories are not readily convertible into cash. First they must be sold and then the debtor/customer has to pay. This renders the current ratio an ineffective or unreliable measure of solvency.

3.2 Acid test (quick ratio)

acid test
A ratio that compares the current assets less stock against the current liabilities, also known as the quick ratio.

quick ratio
Same as current ratio; see working capital ratio (see page 148).

The **acid test** or **quick ratio** is used to examine solvency to overcome the limitation of the current ratio. It is calculated in a similar manner to the working capital ratio, but with one important difference, the exclusion of inventory from the current assets. The acid test is derived as follows:

$$\text{Acid test} = \frac{\text{Current assets less inventories}}{\text{Current liabilities}} : 1$$

A liquidity ratio of 1:1 is desirable in that it affords a company the comfort of knowing it can meet its short-term debts. This does not mean that it is a good ratio, because what is a good ratio will depend upon a range of other factors, such as the sector, the company, its reputation or the economy.

Test yourself 11.2

a) **The following is an extract from J Brown Ltd statement of financial position as at 31 July 20X4.**

Current assets

	£	**£**
Inventory	**5,150**	
Debtors	**1,520**	
Cash	**550**	**7,220**
Current liabilities		
Creditors	**9,086**	
Accruals	**983**	
Bank	**6,120**	**16,189**

Calculate the current and quick ratios for J Brown as at 31 July 20X4.

b) **What is the purpose of the solvency ratios?**

c) **Explain why it may be preferable to use the quick ratio rather than the current ratio.**

4. Working capital management

For **working capital management**, the working capital ratios calculated are designed to examine and assess the use of the company's resources.

working capital management
The ability to management the stock, short-term payables and receivables of a business to ensure the business remains solvent.

4.1 Inventory holding days

Inventory holding days measure how long a company holds its inventory on the shelf. The derivation of the inventory turnover is as follows:

inventory holding days
A ratio that indicates the length of time inventory is held by comparing the average stock level against the cost of sales.

$$\text{Inventory holding days} = \frac{\text{Inventory at the end of the period}}{\text{Cost of goods sold}} \times 365$$

The holding days of inventory is inversely related to the rate of inventory turnover. The longer a company holds its inventories, the slower its turnover rate. Conversely, the shorter a company holds its inventories, the faster its turnover rate. To demonstrate this, consider two identical companies, Omega Ltd and Reema Ltd.

Worked example 11.1

	Omega Ltd	Reema Ltd
Inventory holding days	10	20
Inventory turnover rate	36.5	18.25

The inventory turnover rates resulting from the inventory holding days are derived by dividing the number of days per annum (365) by the number of holding days. Therefore, Reema's holding of its inventory for twice as long as Omega results in a 50% reduction in their inventories.

Holding inventory has associated costs attached, such as the costs of storage, insurance and security, and the risk of obsolescence. This means that the longer a company holds its inventories, the more costly the process is. Therefore a company will seek to minimise its inventory holding days or at least to achieve an optimal holding period.

If the holding days are too long, a company risks obsolescence along with the other direct costs of insurance, security and storage. Similarly, if inventores are held for too short a period, a company may experience shortages as their inventory levels may be insufficient to meet consumer demand. A company will therefore seek to achieve an optimal inventory holding period to minimise either of these problems.

4.2 Collection of trade receivables

The period of credit taken by customers varies between industries. The **collection of trade receivables** measures the time a company takes to collect its debts from its debtors and is calculated in days, as follows:

collection of trade receivables
A ratio that measures how long a business takes to receive payment from its debtors.

$$\text{Collection of trade receivables, in days} = \frac{\text{Trade receivables}}{\text{Credit sales}} \times 365$$

It should be noted that the denominator is confined to credit sales, as only these give rise to debts outstanding. Where the split between cash and credit sales is not given, the total sales figure may be used to calculate the ratio. The ability of a company to collect its trade receivables on time has a direct impact upon its solvency and solvency ratios discussed earlier. As a benchmark, the trade receivables should be the average credit terms of a company.

Changes in the collection of trade receivables may arise from changes in the credit management policies, or discounts granted and taken, or from the fear of penalties for late payment. These changes may be responsible for an improvement or deterioration in the collection of trade receivables.

4.3 Payment of trade payables

payment of trade payables
A ratio that measures how long a business takes to pay its creditors.

This **payment of trade payables** measures the average period of time taken by companies to pay their suppliers and is calculated as follows:

$$\text{Payment of trade payables, in days} = \frac{\text{Trade payables}}{\text{Credit purchases}} \times 365$$

Where the credit purchases are not identifiable in the financial statements, the cost of sales may be used instead.

A change in the rate of payment of suppliers may well reflect an improvement or decline in the solvency position of a company. For instance, if a company is short of cash, it is likely that suppliers will have to wait longer for the payment of amounts due to them. This may be an acceptable short-term strategy.

Changes in payment of trade payables is similar to collection of trade receivables and has a direct relationship with the solvency of a company. A delay in the payment to suppliers may be a policy to improve cash holdings or may result from a worsening in cash balances. Conversely, early payment of suppliers may arise from surplus cash balances or from a desire to maintain a good credit rating.

Test yourself 11.3

The following is an extract from the income statement and statement of financial position of J Brown Ltd at 31 July 20X4.

	£
Sales	**38,000**
Cost of sales	**23,000**
Gross profit	**15,000**
Operating expenses	**9,100**
Profit before interest and taxation	**5,900**

Current assets

	£	**£**
Inventory	**5,150**	
Trade receivables	**1,520**	
Cash	**550**	**7,220**
Current liabilities		
Trade payables	**9,086**	
Accruals	**983**	
Bank	**6,120**	**16,189**

Calculate the following ratios for J Brown plc as at 31 July 20X4:

a) **inventories turnover;**

b) **collection of trade receivables; and**

c) **payment of trade payables.**

5. Gearing

A company may be financed from two sources: equity (shares and reserves, including profit) and debt (loans). The relationship between these two sources combines to provide a level of gearing of a company, i.e how dependent a company is for finance from debt. In addition, there are associated costs of the combination of these finance sources that need to be examined. The relationship between the two financial sources is examined with the aid of the gearing ratio and interest cover ratio.

5.1 Gearing ratio

Gearing is the relationship between equity and debt in the financing of a company and is calculated as follows:

$$\text{Gearing ratio} = \frac{\text{Long-term debt}}{\text{Total capital employed}} \times 100$$

gearing
The relationship between internal (equity) and external (debt) finance in a company's capital structure.

Capital employed is the total of long-term debt plus shareholders' funds. The gearing ratio is a measure of how much of the company's finance comes from external sources. The higher the level of gearing, the greater the risk of a company to the external environment. For example, a company will be more susceptible to changes in interest rates, as interest charges are the cost of the external finance that a company will have to meet annually from its operating profit.

capital employed
The total of the long-term debt and shareholders' funds that is employed in a company to conduct its operational activities.

Companies may be classified as low or highly geared. A gearing level over 50% is regarded as the determinant of a highly geared company. A highly geared company is more exposed to external factors and the risk of insolvency from adverse changes in the external factors. The principal factor is the inability to meet its fixed interest payments. The gearing ratio is complemented by interest cover.

5.2 Interest cover ratio

interest cover
A ratio that measures the ability of a company to finance its interest changes. It is measured by the profit before interest and taxation against the interest payable.

Interest cover measures the ability of a company meeting its interest charges out of its revenue. The interest cover ratio is derived as follows:

$$\text{Interest cover} = \frac{\text{Profit before interest and taxation}}{\text{Interest payable}}$$

The interest cover ratio measures the extent to which the company can cover its fixed interest charges from its operating profit. The ratio is expressed as the number of times and is denoted with '×' after the numerical result.

Worked example 11.2

	31 December 20X4	
	Omega Ltd	**Reema Ltd**
Profit before interest and taxation	£325,790	£256,870
Interest payable	£54,298	£30,220
Interest cover	6×	8.5×

Worked example 11.2 demonstrates the respective interest cover rates for Omega Ltd and Reema Ltd as at 31 December 20X4. As stated above, the interest cover is stated as number of times: 6× versus 8.5×.

The higher the interest cover ratio, the greater a company's ability to meet its interest payment obligations and the less likely its exposure to the risk of insolvency.

Worked example 11.3

Addy Ltd

Income statement for year ending 31 December 20X4

	£
Turnover	1,820,000
Cost of sales	1,314,300
Gross profit	505,700
Operating expenses	387,015
Profit before interest and taxation	118,685
Interest payable	11,050
Pre-tax profit	107,635

Addy Ltd

Statement of financial position at 31 December 20X4

	£	£	£
Non-current assets			2,039,100
Current assets			
Inventories	128,400		
Receivables	85,750		
Bank		231,210	
	17,060		
Current liabilities			
Payables		116,575	
Net current assets			114,635
Long-term liabilities			
Long-term debt			1,000,000
Net assets			1,153,735
Capital and reserves			
Ordinary shares			1,028,000
Revenue reserves			125,735
Shareholders' funds			1,153,735

With the use of suitable accounting ratios for the year ending 31 December, comment on Addy's following performances:

a) profit margins;

b) solvency;

c) management of working capital; and

d) gearing

Answer

a) Profit margins

Gross profit margin $\frac{\text{Gross profit}}{\text{Turnover}} \times 100$ 27.79%

Operating profit margin $\frac{\text{Operating profit}}{\text{Turnover}} \times 100$ 6.52%

Addy is generating a gross profit of £27.79 per £100 of sales as measured by the gross profit margin. However, once all the operating costs are covered, Addy has an annual profit of £6.52. Therefore, the overheads of the company are consuming £21.27 per £100 of sales.

b) Solvency

Current ratio	Current assets: Current liabilities	1.98:1
Quick ratio	Current assets less inventory: Current liabilities	0.88:1

Addy is able to meet its current obligations as shown by a 1.98:1 current ratio. However, when inventory are removed, the quick convertible assets are less able to meet their short-term obligation, as the ratio is less than 1:1.

c) Management of working capital

Inventory holding days $\frac{\text{Inventory}}{\text{Credit sales}} \times 365$ 35.65 days

Collection of trade receivables $\frac{\text{Receivables}}{\text{Sales}} \times 365$ 17.20 days

Payment of trade payables $\frac{\text{Payables}}{\text{Cost of sales}} \times 365$ 32.37 days

Credit sales and purchases are not provided, therefore the total sales and cost of sales are used to calculate the collection of trade receivables and payment of trade payables ratios.

Addy's inventory turns over at least once per month, or 14 times per annum. The company is more effective at collecting its payables (17 days) than paying its payables (32 days). Addy is taking almost twice as long to pay its payables as it takes to collect its own debts.

d) Gearing

Gearing ratio $\frac{\text{Long-term debt}}{\text{Capital employed}} \times 100$ 46.30%

Interest cover $\frac{\text{Profit before interest and taxation}}{\text{Interest payable}}$ 10.74%

Addy has a gearing ratio less than 50%, therefore it is not regarded as highly geared. In addition, Addy is able to meet its interest payments over ten times from its operating profit.

It is not possible to provide a holistic opinion about Addy. The additional information that would assist in the provision of a holistic analysis include:

a) non financial information such as: the set targets or goals for the accounting ratios, its business sector and the nature of the economy.

b) financial information about Addy's performance in the last two to four years plus comparative financial results for the performance of other firms in the sector.

6. The limitations of accounting ratios

The various accounting ratios seek to provide users of financial statements with a greater understanding of a company's performance. However, the accounting ratios suffer from a number of limitations that should be borne in mind by anyone attempting to interpret their significance. The main limitations are as follows:

- The ratios do not provide explanations for observed changes, and the external user's ability to obtain further information varies considerably.
- A deterioration in an accounting ratio cannot necessarily be interpreted as poor management.
- Too much significance should not be attached to individual ratios. For example, a gross profit margin of 60% might indicate that all is well, but this conclusion might be unjustified if further analysis revealed a solvency ratio of 0.4:1.
- Company financial statements are usually based on historic events, therefore ratios provide a further understanding of past events. They are not always useful for a forward-looking or planning tool.
- Accounting policies such as depreciation of non-current assets may affect the annual financial statements and as such the resulting accounting ratios.
- Consideration must be given to variations in commercial trading patterns when assessing the significance of accounting ratios computed for particular companies. For example, a retail chain of supermarkets would be expected to have a much lower liquidity ratio and a much higher rate of inventory turnover than a constructional engineering firm. In this context, accepted 'norms' such as a working capital ratio of 2:1 must be used with care.

Test yourself 11.4

Outline three problems that may arise when comparing the accounting ratios of two companies.

Chapter summary

- Accounting ratios are used to interpret and explain the performance of a company beyond the static financial statements.
- The key financial ratios are as follows:

Profit margins

Gross profit margin $\frac{\text{Gross profit}}{\text{Sales}} \times 100$

Net profit margin $\frac{\text{Operating profit}}{\text{Sales}} \times 100$

Solvency

Current ratio $= \frac{\text{Current assets}}{\text{Current liabilities}} : 1$

Acid test $= \frac{\text{Current assets less inventories}}{\text{Current liabilities}} : 1$

Working capital management

Inventory holding days $\frac{\text{Inventory at the end of the period}}{\text{Cost of sales}} \times 365$

Collection of trade receivables $\frac{\text{Trade receivables}}{\text{Sales}} \times 365$

Payment of trade payables $\frac{\text{Trade payables}}{\text{Cost of sales}} \times 365$

Gearing

Gearing ratio $\frac{\text{Long-term debt}}{\text{Capital employed}} \times 100$

Interest cover $\frac{\text{Profit before interest and taxation}}{\text{Interest payable}}$ 10.74%

- Profit margins can be used to explain a company's performance in relation to its cost of sales or its total operating expenses.
- Solvency ratios explain the ability of a company to meet its short-term obligations.

- The current ratio as a measure of solvency suffers from the deficiency of inventory included within the current assets.
- The management of working capital ratios examines a company's ability to use its resources to collect its trade receivables and pay its trade payables in a timely manner.
- Inventory holding days is a measure of the speed at which a company converts its inventory into sales.
- The gearing ratio examines the relationship between internal and external financing of a company.
- Accounting ratios aid comparative company performance over time, versus competitors' performance and versus benchmarks or the company's own goals.
- Accounting ratio guides, such as the current ratio 2:1, must not be regarded as fixed laws.
- Accounting ratios do not explain why changes have occurred.
- Accounting ratios can be affected by a company's accounting policy, such as depreciation.
- Accounting ratios are useful tools to provide an understanding of the financial statements for comparative purposes; they are not useful on their own, or in isolation from other information.

Test yourself answers

Test yourself 11.1

a) D – Sales

b) C – £9,600

c) C – 39.47%

Test yourself 11.2

a) Current ratio 0.45:1
Quick ratio 0.13:1

b) The purpose of solvency ratios is to provide a general guide to inform readers of financial statements whether a company (or organisation) can meet its short-term debts.

c) The quick ratio is deemed a better measure of solvency than the current ratio because it excludes the inventories in its computation.

Test yourself 11.3

a) Inventories turnover $\dfrac{365}{\text{Inventory holding days}}$

Inventory holding days $\dfrac{\text{Closing inventory}}{\text{Cost of goods sold}} \times 365$

Inventory holding days $\dfrac{5{,}150}{23{,}000} \times 365$

81.73

Inventories turnover $\dfrac{365}{81.73}$

4.47 times per year

b) Collection of trade receivables $\dfrac{\text{Trade receivables}}{\text{Sales}} \times 365$

$\dfrac{1{,}520}{38{,}000} \times 365$

14.6 days

c) Payment of trade payables $\dfrac{\text{Trade creditors}}{\text{Cost of sales}} \times 365$

$\dfrac{9{,}086}{23{,}000} \times 365$

144.19 days

Test yourself 11.4

1. The companies may have different accounting year-end dates – for example, 31 March 20X4 and 30 September 20X4. This prevents a true comparative analysis.
2. The companies may apply different accounting treatment to items of their property, plant and equipment. The companies may use either different methods of depreciation or they may use the same methods but assign different economic lives to the items of property, plant and equipment.
3. The companies may be in different business sectors or geographical location and consequently have different company strategies and/or encounter different operating environments.

Glossary

Accounting period The period for which the financial statements have been prepared.

Accounting ratios The relationship between two or more items from the financial statements.

Accruals Costs that have not so far been taken into account at the end of a period because they have not yet been invoiced but are to be invoiced in arrears – for example, gas or electricity.

Accrued expense An expense that has been incurred and the benefit received during an accounting period which remains unpaid at the end of the accounting period.

Acid test A ratio that compares the current assets less stock against the current liabilities, also known as the quick ratio.

Asset Any tangible or intangible possession that has value.

Bad debt A debt that is or is considered to be uncollectible and is, therefore, written off as a charge to the profit and loss account.

Balance sheet A statement of the financial position of an entity at a given date, disclosing the assets, liabilities and accumulated funds.

Bank reconciliation A process of comparing the bank statement balance with the cash book balance.

Book of prime entry A first record of transactions, such as sales or purchases, from which details or totals, as appropriate, are transferred to the ledgers.

Business entity concept The principle that financial accounting information relates only to the activities of the business entity and not to the activities of its owner(s).

Capital employed The total of the long-term debt and shareholders' funds that is employed in a company to conduct its operational activities.

Capital expenditure Expenditure that is likely to provide a benefit to the organisation for more than one accounting period/financial year.

Capital income The proceeds of selling fixed assets.

Capital The funds used by an entity for its operations.

Cash book A book that records the cash accounts of a business.

Collection of trade receivables A ratio that measures how long a business takes to receive payment from its debtors.

Consistency The principle that there is uniformity of accounting treatment of like items within each accounting period and from one period to the next.

Control account An account that provides an arithmetic check of a ledger.

Cost of sales The sum of variable cost of sales plus factory overhead attributable to the turnover. It may also be referred to as production cost of sales or cost of goods sold.

Credit An entry on the right-hand side of an account in double-entry bookkeeping that denotes an income in the profit and loss account or a liability in the balance sheet.

Creditors Persons or businesses to whom money is owed.

Current assets Assets that will change their form in a short period of time.

Current liabilities Persons or businesses to whom money is owed and falls due and payable within 12 months.

Current ratio *See* **working capital ratio**.

Debit An entry on the left-hand side of an account in the double-entry bookkeeping that denotes an expense in the profit and loss account or an asset in the balance sheet.

Debtors Persons or businesses who owe money to a business.

Depreciation The measure of wearing out, consumption or other reduction in the useful economic life of a fixed asset.

Double entry A method of recording transactions in ledger accounts so that the monetary value of the debits and credits always balance each other.

Drawings Monies or goods taken out of the business by a sole trader for private use.

Expenses The expenses of operating the business for the accounting period.

Financial statements A set of documents produced by a business to show financial performance and position of the business, including a trading profit and loss account and a balance sheet.

Fixed assets Assets owned by an entity with a lifespan greater than 12 months.

Gearing The relationship between internal (equity) and external (debt) finance in a company's capital structure.

Going concern The assumption that the entity will continue in operational existence for the foreseeable future.

Gross profit margin A ratio that reflects the gross profit as a percentage of the sales for a business.

Gross profit Sales less the cost of goods sold.

Historic cost concept The principle that resources are normally stated in accounts at the amount that was paid to acquire them.

Imprest system A method of controlling cash or stock; when the cash or stock has been reduced by disbursements or issues, it is restored to its original level.

Income and expenditure account An annual financial statement for a non-profit-making organisation that reflects the surplus or deficit made during the accounting period.

Intangible fixed assets A group of fixed assets owned by an entity with a lifespan greater than 12 months that do not have a physical existence; they cannot be seen or touched.

Interest cover A ratio that measures the ability of a company to finance its interest changes. It is measured by the profit before interest and taxation against the interest payable.

International Financial Reporting Standards A set of principles-based standards, interpretations and framework for financial statements.

Inventory holding days A ratio that indicates the length of time inventory is held by comparing the average stock level against the cost of sales.

Journal A record of financial transactions, such as transfers between accounts, not dealt with elsewhere.

Liability The financial obligations of a business, e.g. creditors, bank and overdrafts.

Limited company A business owned by shareholders with their liability limited to their share capital.

Long-term liabilities Persons or businesses to whom money is owed and the debt is payable beyond 12 months.

Materiality The principle that financial statements should disclose items separately that are significant enough to affect evaluation or decisions.

Money measurement concept The principle that financial accounting information relates only to those activities that can be expressed in money terms.

Net assets The excess of book value of assets over liabilities, including loan capital.

Net book value The historic cost of an asset less any accumulated depreciation or other provision for the diminution in value, e.g. reduction to net realisable value.

Net profit Gross profit less operational expenses.

Net profit margin A ratio that reflects the net profit as a percentage of the sales for a business.

Net realisable value The sales value of stock that an organisation expects to receive when the stock is sold. This may be lesser or greater than the cost of the stock owing to deterioration, obsolescence or appreciation over time.

Nominal ledger A ledger for impersonal accounts.

Non-current assets *See* **fixed assets**.

Non-current liabilities *See* **long-term liabilities**.

Not-for-profit organisation A non-commercial organisation that does not exist in order to make a profit and is unable to distribute any of its annual surplus to its members.

Owner's capital The total of the original capital invested by the owner in the business, plus any retained profits or reserves from previous years, plus this year's profits less any drawings made by the owner during the year.

Partnership A business where ownership is shared among two or more people.

Payment of trade payables A ratio that measures how long a business takes to pay its creditors.

Periodicity concept The period for which a set of business activities is reported in the financial statement.

Petty cash account A record of relatively small cash receipts and payments, the balance representing the cash in the control of an individual, usually dealt with under an imprest system.

Petty cash book A book for recording receipts and payments made out of a petty cash account.

Prepayment Expenditure on goods or services for future benefit, which is to be charged to future operations, e.g. rentals paid in advance.

Profit and loss account A statement that shows the income less the various expenses of an organisation, to show the profit or loss for an accounting period.

Provision for doubtful debts A provision made for debtors that may be uncollectable at the balance sheet date.

Prudence The principle that income is included in the financial statements only when realised, while likely losses are included as soon as possible.

Public listed companies Limited companies whose shares are available to be purchased by the general public.

Purchase ledger control account A ledger control account that records the totals of entries in the individual creditors' ledger. This is also known as the creditors control account.

Purchase return Goods returned by a business to its supplier.

Purchases or creditors ledger A ledger for a supplier's personal account.

Purchases Raw materials purchased for incorporation into products or finished goods purchased for resale.

Quick ratio Same as current ratio; *see* **working capital ratio**.

Reducing-balance method A method of depreciation that reduces annually over the life of the fixed asset.

Retained profits Non-distributed profits retained as revenue reserve. In a not-for-profit entity, these are described as accumulated funds.

Revenue expenditure Expenditure on the supply and manufacture of goods and provision of services charged in the accounting period in which they are consumed.

Revenue income Amounts derived from the provision of goods and services falling within the company's ordinary activities, after deduction of returns, trade discounts and value added tax; also called turnover/sales.

Revenue recognition concept The recording of revenue in the books of accounts in the appropriate accounting period. Revenue is recognised when the buyer assumes ownership and title of the goods.

Sales ledger control account A ledger control account that records the totals of entries in the individual debtors ledger. This is also known as the debtors ledger control account.

Sales or debtors ledger A collection of the accounts or records receivable from each customer.

Sales return Goods returned to a business by its customers.

Settlement discount A reduction in an invoice granted to a customer in exchange for early payment.

Sole trader A person carrying on business with sole legal responsibility for the business, not in partnership or as a company.

Solvency The ability of a business to pay its short-term debts as they become due and payable.

Source documents Documents that contain the information that is put into an accounting system.

Stable monetary unit concept The use of monetary units to report items in financial statements. This permits nominal comparative analysis, although the monetary unit may not maintain a constant value.

Stakeholders Those with interests in an organisation.

Stock Stocks are made up of goods purchased for resale. The intention is to resell the stock, so it will normally be kept in the business for a relatively short time.

Straight-line method A method of depreciation that remains fixed over the life of the fixed asset.

Substance over form Transactions are accounted for by their commercial reality rather than legal form.

Tangible fixed assets A group of fixed assets owned by an entity with a lifespan greater than 12 months with a physical existence.

Trade discount A reduction in selling price given to customer at the point of sales.

Trial balance A list of account balances in a double-entry accounting system.

Units of constant purchasing power concept During exceptional periods of hyperinflation, all non-monetary items are to be restated in terms of the consumer price index as at the end of the accounting period. This seeks to maintain the capital purchasing power during inflationary and deflationary periods.

Working capital The capital available for conducting the day-to-day operations of an organisation; normally the excess of current assets over current liabilities.

Working capital management The ability to management the stock, short-term payables and receivables of a business to ensure the business remains solvent.

Working capital ratio A ratio that compares the current assets against the current liabilities. Also known as the current ratio.

Write off Reduce the value of an asset to nil on a balance sheet.

Directory of web resources

Professional bodies

The Association of Accounting Technicians
www.aat.org.uk

The Association of Chartered Certified Accountants
www.accaglobal.com

The Chartered Institute of Management Accountants
www.cimaglobal.com

The Chartered Institute of Public Finance and Accountancy
www.cipfa.org.uk (not-for-profit body)

The Institute of Chartered Accountants in England and Wales
www.icaew.com

Index

www.ingramcontent.com/pod-product-compliance
Ingram Content Group UK Ltd.
Pitfield, Milton Keynes, MK11 3LW, UK
UKHW051928100926
8556IPUK00022B/1436

9 781860 727313